D0949289

Original Love

~~~~~~~~~~~~~~~~

Des Cummings, Jr.

HART BOOKS
A Ministry of Hart Research Center
FALLBROOK, CALIFORNIA

Unless otherwise noted, scripture quotations are from the New American Standard
Bible, copyright © 1960, 1962, 1963, 1971, 1972, 1973, 1975, 1977, 1994 by The
Lockman Foundation. Used by permission.

Texts credited to NEB are from The New English Bible. © The Delegates of the
Oxford University Press and the Syndics of the Cambridge University Press, 1961,
1970. Reprinted by permission.

Texts credited to NKJV are from the New King James Version. Copyright © 1979,
1980, 1982 by Thomas Nelson, Inc. Used by permission. All rights reserved.

Editing and page composition: Ken McFarland
Cover art direction and design: Mark Bond, Mark Bond Design

ISBN: 1-878046-58-6

Contents

Dedication 4

Acknowledgments 5

Foreword 7

Introduction 9

1. The Lesson of Eden 11

2. The Primary Colors of Love 15

3. The Primary Colors of Sin 25

4. How to Experience Original Love 37

   Experiencing Sabbath Advance Planning 43

The Journey to Rest

5. Restless in Ur 49

6. The Halfway Hazard—Stuck in Haran 55

7. Grand Expectations 59

8. Egypt 63

9. Egypt in My Home 69

10. The Last Laugh 75

11. Snickers From the Kitchen 81

12. The Promise Fulfilled 85

13. The Birth of Isaac 91

14. Home at Last 93

15. God's View of Moriah 101

    Experiencing Sabbath Rest 105

The Journey to Blessing

16. The Sabbath Is Heaven's Hug 111

17. A Bad Beginning 115

18. A Woman Shamed 121

19. Living the Blessing in the Land of Cursing 131

    Experiencing Sabbath Blessing 137

The Journey to Sanctification

20. A Family Divided 143

21. Human Wrongs 149

22. New Beginnings 153

23. Making a Nation Great 159

24. Seeing Providence in Pain 171

25. Finally Family 175

    Experiencing Sabbath Sanctification 183

Dedication

I DEDICATE THIS BOOK TO:

Mary Lou, my loving gift from God. She has made this book practical through her commitment to recreating Sabbath in our family every week and sharing her ideas in the life application chapters. She has made it more readable through hours of editing. She has made Sabbath a delight through her magnetic enthusiasm and abundant joy. Mary Lou, I look forward to celebrating Sabbath with you forever.

Our children, Tracy and Derek, who are living examples that God still works miracles. You have embraced the Sabbath and enhanced its practice in our home. The Lord has used both of you to expand my understanding of Him. I am thankful that you and your life partners Denis and Vivian will teach Sabbath to the next generation.

My parents, Elder Des and Lois Cummings, who first introduced me to God's love. My father is a minister; I was his first baptism and continue to be his greatest admirer. My mother is a teacher; I was her first child. She mentored me in the ways of God, and I continue to be her greatest fan. Together Mom and Dad taught my sisters (Candace Neal and Paula Wade), and I the Christian values that have shaped our lives. I am eternally grateful.

Acknowledgments

I WOULD LIKE TO acknowledge the following people and organizations who have contributed to the development of this book:

Jesus, who called me to His love, caused me to become a new creature, and the Spirit who taught me that love is the norm for interpreting scripture.

Mary Lou's parents, Walter and Birdie Parker, who loved me like a son and her family who love me like a brother. This love continues to provide me with encouragement and inspiration.

The Cummings, Brody–Knutson, extended family that has surrounded me with relatives who share Christian values and provide Godly role models.

Tom Werner, President of the Adventist Health System, who invited me to join Florida Hospital and challenged me to explain the benefits of Sabbath to new employees. He later supported my efforts to design Florida Hospital Celebration Health around the health principles of creation.

Don Jernigan, President of Florida Hospital, who affirmed my interpretation of Sabbath and encouraged me to put the principles into a book.

To the Celebration Health and Spiritual Life planning teams for their friendship and dedication that manifest itself in hours of prayer, discussion, and debate that matured my thinking about creation week

To Donna Burske, who read, and corrected the first draft.

To my Sabbath School class, "The Firm," for being a focus group for me to test the concepts in this book and whose friendship, spiritual depth, intellectual honesty, and Christian love continue to draw me closer to God.

To the Seventh-day Adventist Church for the heritage of Sabbath that provided me with a secure platform of truth from which I could build a home and ministry. For the youth ministry of the church that taught me that joy of knowing Jesus. For an education system that taught me to love God and study scripture. And for the health ministry that enabled me to interface with society and learn what it means to "live in the world but not of the world."

For the writings of Jewish and Christian authors who have studied the Sabbath and enlarged it's meaning to me.

Foreword

IN A SOCIETY THAT IS love-starved, Des Cummings writes with creative, refreshing insight. His down-to-earth, practical, biblical narrative speaks to all of our hearts. Des writes of the God who loves unconditionally.

Original Love is a one-of-a-kind volume. It takes us back to the beginning—the origin of all things. It speaks of a God who created life over six days, but on the seventh created love. Des Cummings presents the Sabbath of creation in an invigorating new way. For Des and his wife, Mary Lou, the Sabbath is a day for relationships—relationships with each other, relationships with their children, and relationships with God. In a frenzied world, *Original Love* speaks of a God who in the Sabbath gives us His peaceful rest, the richness of His blessing, and His joy of harmonious living. You will especially appreciate Mary Lou's warm touch in sharing practical, creative ways on how to make Sabbath everything God wants it to be in your own home.

Scores of books come across my desk each week. This one is amazingly different. Its concepts are innovative and will make a real difference in your life, as they have in mine. I have known Des Cummings for twenty years. He is an original thinker who writes from the depths of his own experience, with a real passion for people. This book will speak to the heart of your acceptance by God and increase your self-esteem as you read it. You will find yourself turning to its pages again an again for hope, encouragement, and spiritual strength. I'm convinced that this refreshing book will be the blessing to you that it has been to me. I highly recommend it.

Mark Finley
Speaker/Director
It Is Written International Television

Introduction

***ORIGINAL LOVE* IS ALL ABOUT** rediscovering the essence of the creation Sabbath. For Mary Lou and me, this process began several years ago with a fresh look at the creation story. We are now convinced that the way to live life to the fullest is to understand the Creator's original design and purpose. The first section of this book is devoted to sharing the insights we have discovered—insights summarized in the premise that "in six days God created life, and on the seventh day God created love."

The message of the seventh day of creation is that God set apart a full day of dedicated time to grow love with His children. We decided that if the Sabbath was vital to love in a perfect world, it was even more critical in a fallen world. Based on this belief, we began to reshape our family life around the practice of Sabbath.

Sabbath became the focal point of our week! We began to plan each Sabbath around experiencing *Rest, Blessing,* and *Sanctification.* We began to refer to these three Sabbath concepts as the Primary Colors of Love. They became the focus of our study. And the more we discovered their meaning, the more we found ways to plan Sabbath experiences (activities) that recaptured their power. Mary Lou outlines some of these activities that have enriched our family following each section of the book on one of love's primary colors.

To help you implement these activities in your own family, we have videotaped them. This video is titled *Original Love in Action.* Ordering information is on page 186.

I began to realize that both the New Testament and the Old Testament are built on the foundation of two of God's great acts of love. The New Testament is built on the reclaiming of life through the great love act of the cross. Over the years godly professors have taught me beautiful lessons by helping me view the New Testament through the cross.

The more I studied the creation story, the more I became convinced that the Old Testament is built on the creation of life through the love act of the Sabbath. I have come to believe that the best way to understand the Old Testament is to view it through the Sabbath. When I reached this conclusion, I began to reexamine the stories of the patriarchs.

In the stories of Abraham and Sarah, Jacob and Leah, Joseph and Aseneth, I found God infusing the principles of Sabbath into the life and worship of His chosen nation. The lives of each of these patriarchal couples reveal the power of one of the dimensions of Sabbath. A major part of this book is devoted to sharing their journeys, because I believe they provide us with insight into how the Sabbath can lead us to redemption in our fallen world:

Abraham and Sarah journey to **Rest.**

Jacob and Leah journey to **Blessing.**

Joseph and Aseneth journey to **Sanctification.**

God is consistently at work to fulfill His original plan for love by embedding it in the creation week, in the forebears of a nation, in His ministry of redemption, and in the Church. If you want to live life to its fullest today, journey back to the Garden and discover how God intended to gift humans with love.

1

The Lesson of Eden

THE STORY OF CREATION reveals the drama of a universe in the making, and as the Master Designer steps to center stage to conduct a symphony of love, the first five days are devoted to creating the setting for God's children. The power of His work reveals itself in cosmic blasts that send planets into space and set the nights aglow. Day by day God conducts the next movement of creative magnificence, from the forming of the animals to the landscape architecture of the garden.

As I returned to the creation story, I asked myself, "What is the plot of this story? What is God telling us about life and its origin?" As I studied the first two chapters of Genesis, I began to identify with the Creator—and here's why. I found that the genius of this story is that it is a drama—not a documentary. It is all about a God who is preparing for the arrival of His children, and Eden is the nursery.

This is the story of a loving Father creating the perfect place in which His children could play. It is not about power but about people. It is not about science but about serenity. The story is something we can relate to because we have lived all the instincts of

Eden. They are embedded in the human experience of procreation.

I remember when Mary Lou and I were told that we were going to have a baby. The parenting instincts immediately responded, and we started to gather things together in preparation for the baby. Creating a nursery was our focus.

I believe what God was doing in the first six days of creation was preparing the nursery in which He would place His children, to enjoy the experience of living in love as a family. When we prepared for the arrival of our baby, the first thing we did was to decorate a special room in the house. Our creative activity mirrored God's.

The only difference lay in two words—*power* and *budget.* God had an unlimited power and budget. We had limited power and budget.

The first thing that we did in preparation for our baby was to go and look for a carpet for the floor of the nursery. Now, I'll have to admit that I went to a discount store to buy a carpet. I found a great buy on a carpet remnant. My wife called it cheap. I preferred to think of it as economical.

God didn't put cheap (economical) carpet on the floor of His garden. He laid down the lush grass of the earth—a padding of thick turf designed for the bare feet of His children. And as they ran, they would know that He had been there before, making sure everything was right.

We chose wallpaper with a pattern of butterflies, flowers, and blue sky. God didn't put pictures of butterflies and flowers on His walls. He created the real thing. We put stuffed animals in the crib. He created a petting zoo filled with a vast variety of living animals that would delight His children. Our nursery was ten feet wide and twelve feet long—but His encompassed a universe. Yet I would submit to you that we were both doing the same thing—experiencing the same excitement and feeling the same anticipation. We were getting ready to have children and doing our best to make sure they would know they are loved.

We were told by the doctor that a mobile would help the baby's eyes to develop properly, so we bought a mobile of plastic birds that circled to music. God filled the air with birds of every shape and color and then gifted each with their own song to create a symphony.

When we put the last item in place, we stepped back and smiled. This was as good as we could do, and we were pleased. Only one thing remained—the arrival of our baby. God did the same thing, except that He was able to say that it was very good. Only one thing remained—the arrival of His children.

Now as He comes to the sixth day of creation, the universe watches as He speaks the animals into existence. The only thing remaining is the creation of humans. This will not be done by simple command. God chooses to sculpt His children in His own image with His own hands. He kneels on the ground, and with the care of a father and the intimacy of a mother, He molds Adam into His likeness. And then, as if kissing him into being, Jesus breathes into him the breath of life.

As Adam becomes a living soul, the moment is as dramatic as that in any delivery room as he looks into the eyes of his heavenly Father. The waiting room of heaven is filled with angel faces pressed to the glass to catch the first words of the first human.

Father and child walk and talk through the nursery, and Adam is given the opportunity to see what God has created. Finally, as if turning over the keys to a new car, the heavenly Father invites Adam to enter into the creative joy of naming the animals. It is a delightful process and one that confirms his role as "king of the world." As Adam goes through the process of naming, he notices that the animals all have companions—all, that is, except him.

And for the first time in the creation story, God says it's not good! There is discord in the symphonic score. The problem is clear—it is not good that a man should be alone. Perhaps God allowed Adam to experience the absence of companionship so that when Eve was created, he would cherish her.

God put Adam to sleep and performed the first surgery. With the same intimate care, He sculpted the perfect woman.

As God awakened Adam from surgery, He introduced Eve to him, and it was "love at first sight." This was one of the most powerful moments in the creation experience. It was filled with wonder and romance as the wonder of human love filled their hearts. Adam described the power of human love: "For this cause, a man shall leave his father and his mother, and shall cleave to his wife."Genesis 2:24.

At that point in time, he didn't know who his father and mother were, but he knew that he must cleave to this woman, for she was bone of his bone and flesh of his flesh. Most of all, she was the complement to his life, and together they would live in love.

Now, I have to tell you, if I were writing the story of creation for a Hollywood movie, I would close it with the wedding of Adam and Eve and the establishment of family. What an incredible finale! What a romantic ending!

Think of it. The first wedding on earth. God has all the resources of heaven to plan this wedding. The angel choir to create the music. He could cast a rainbow over the Tree of Life for the backdrop and setting for the ceremony. He could have an animal parade lead the couple to the tree, and the birds could drop flower petals from the sky to decorate the path.

And at the moment of the kiss, the fountains could explode, and the angel choir could sing a song of love that would never be forgotten. It would be magnificent!

So when I looked at the creation story and thought of how well it could have ended with the marriage of Adam and Eve on Friday night, I was compelled to ask why a seventh day, and what purpose does it serve?

For in fact, God doesn't create anything on this day. He simply takes the day off to be with Adam and Eve.

And then it struck me—this is the day for love, and I realized that everything that God was doing during the first six days of creation was made meaningful on the seventh day. For you see, in six days God created life, and on the seventh day He created love. Life without love is like sheet music without a symphony. There is no melody. Life without love is existence, but life filled with love is Sabbath.

I would suggest to you that the Sabbath was the day on which God sculptured original love.

2

The Primary Colors of Love

"BY THE SEVENTH DAY God completed His work which He had done, and He rested from all His work which He had done. God blessed the seventh day and sanctified it." Genesis 2:2, 3.

Over the first six days, God did good work, but on the seventh day, He established perfection by stopping all His work to focus on the best thing in life—love. Seven is the biblical number that represents perfection. This designation is derived from Sabbath, the perfect day.

It was perfect because it embodied the purpose of creation. On the sixth day God created Adam and Eve, joined them in love, and called it marriage. On the seventh day God created a day for love, united them with Himself, and called it Sabbath.

Sabbath is heaven's heartbeat. God gave His children an unforgettable day of undivided attention. On this day He revealed the three dimensions of love. Scripture defines them as Rest, Blessing, and Sanctification. I think of them as the primary colors of love. Like red, yellow, and blue, they form the basis of all the many colors of love. These three elements of Sabbath form the primary pallet from which God blends all the shades of virtue.

The more we understand these eternal principles, the more we can experience love now and forever. These principles not only guaranteed love in the perfect world of the garden, but they are key to your ability to experience love today.

Rest: The First Color of Love

By sundown on the sixth day, God has completed His work. Like an artist surveying a masterpiece, He steps back and declares that it is very good. Good work is satisfying, and God enjoys His work. But work must stop in order to have Sabbath.

Both in the Garden and at the Cross, God completes His work on Friday. From the Garden, He pronounces it completed and then enters into Sabbath rest. From the Cross He pronounces that "It is finished" and enters into Sabbath rest. On both occasions He has brought life to humanity. In the Garden He created life with His breath, and on the Cross He redeemed life with His blood. In both cases the universe needed to stop and spend time absorbing God's love. In short, they needed Sabbath rest.

Rest is the first of the primary colors of love that God embedded in the Sabbath. The most common meaning of the Hebrew word for rest is "to cease" or "stop." On the first Sabbath God rested from His work—He stopped. Stopping has no real value in and of itself. In fact, it can be detrimental, leading to boredom and the idea that holiness is best experienced in isolation from the world. The value of stopping is to put an end to one activity to focus on something else. In the case of Sabbath, God stopped creating to focus on His creatures.

The second dimension of rest is to realize that God has completed all the work needed to provide you with eternal life. Your life is guaranteed by His work. Draw close to Him, and you will sense the confidence that comes from knowing an all-powerful Father.

David summarized, "Relax [stop] and know [draw close] that I am God [Victor]." (See Psalm 46:10.) A paraphrase could read, "Slow down and stop—look at Me. I love you and want to take away everything that makes you anxious. Rest for a day and understand that I am God, that I have won the war and will fight for you! You can live with confidence." Perhaps if David were writing to us in today's Internet language, he might say to us, "For true rest, log on to: God.calm."

As a father, I know what rest really means to my children. I experienced it when my son, Derek, was learning to sleep by himself. He was born underweight and needed special care. He slept in a cradle beside our bed, and when he cried, my wife would pick him up and let him sleep in bed beside her. When he was in our bed, he always slept better. This became a habit, and he couldn't seem to go to sleep without one of us lying down beside him. This went on until he was almost three years old, when we decided it was time for him to learn to go to sleep by himself.

We told Derek that he was a big boy now and needed to sleep in his own bed by himself. His response was, "Daddy, I'm afraid of the dark."

I came up with what I thought was a simple but elegant solution. It was a plan to replace a human sleeping companion with a teddy bear. Not just an ordinary bear, but one that had a personality with which my son could bond. I searched for such a bear and felt very proud when I found an English bear named Paddington. The bear was personified through a series of storybooks, and we began to read them to Derek. By the time we came to the sixth and last book, he had become enchanted with the antics of Paddington.

Now it was time to commence our plan. I announced to Derek that starting the next week, he would be a "big boy" and sleep with Paddington. He nodded his head and repeated, "Daddy, next week I will be a big boy and sleep with Paddington."

The appointed night came, and Derek began to exhibit signs of anxiety. As we got ready for bed, he made me check under his bed and in his closet for scary creatures of the night. I patiently did all this and read him his story. He pressed especially close to me as we had prayer.

When I tucked Paddington into bed beside him, he looked up at me and asked, "Daddy, won't you lie down beside me while I go to sleep?"

I responded, "Derek, you have Paddington beside you, and you're going to be a 'big boy' tonight."

I kissed him good night and even kissed the bear, hoping that might give my furry substitute more credibility. "Mom and I will be in the family room reading if you need us," I said as I exited the room quickly before a second appeal.

I entered the family room and gave Mary Lou the "thumbs up" sign. I picked up the paper and began to read, pleased with the way the plan was working. The quiet lasted for all of thirty seconds, and then a tiny voice called from the bedroom.

"Daddy?"

"Yes, Derek?"

"Daddy, I'm scared."

"Derek, there is nothing to be scared about. Just go to sleep with Paddington."

A few minutes of silence, and then, "Daddy, I need a drink of water."

"Derek, you've already had a drink. It's time to go to sleep."

A few more minutes of silence, and then, "Daddy, I need to go to the bathroom."

Now he had raised *my* anxiety, and I took him to the bathroom. We returned to his bedroom and repeated the "good night" ritual of hugs and kisses. I was ready to leave, when he looked up at me and said, "Daddy, would you lie down with me? I'm afraid!"

"Derek, there is no need to be afraid. Mommy and I are in the other room, and Paddington is right here beside you."

I looked down at his eyes wide with fear, and then Derek said something I will never forget.

"But Daddy, Paddington doesn't have skin!"

Every father wants his children to be able to rest in his love. This same protective desire was built into Sabbath. I slipped into bed beside Derek and watched as his eyes returned to rest. I whispered, "I love you, Buddy," and he responded, "I'll be a 'big boy' tomorrow night, Daddy."

Sabbath is God's security blanket for His children.

God gave us a perfect example of how to practice rest. He stopped everything else and spent a full day getting to know Adam and Eve. The first Sabbath must have been filled with unforgettable memories.

The three prerequisites necessary in order for us to experience the Sabbath rest as modeled by God are:

1. Stop working.

2. Relax, knowing your work is completed in Christ.

3. Bring your family together to grow love. Sabbath and family are indissolubely linked together. This is why we dedicate Sabbath to worship and family.

Blessing: The Second Color of Love

Blessing has two meanings. The first meaning is "favored by God." One of the greatest examples of this occurred when God gave Moses the words the priests were to say in greeting the people of Israel as they come to worship Him.

"Thus you shall bless the sons of Israel. You shall say to them: The Lord bless you, and keep you; The Lord make His face shine on you, and be gracious to you; The Lord lift up His countenance on you, and give you peace." Numbers 6:23-26.

It is a Jewish tradition to begin the Sabbath by blessing the children in the home. This is traced to the creation story. The thought is that God began Sabbath by taking Adam and Eve into His arms and telling them how much He loved them. You can imagine a very personal version of the blessing above:

"Adam and Eve, I look at you and smile. I'm so thankful that you are My children. I love you so much that I want to give you every good gift. Most of all, I want to be with you all the time and make sure you are satisfied with life."

The second meaning of blessing is "to kneel down and kiss." This is an act of humans toward God, signifying honor and worship. Through a Sabbath blessing, God brings worth and favor to our lives, and we return worship and honor to Him. Thus, we bless one another. We are filled with worth, and we overflow with praise. Nehemiah realized the importance of Sabbath blessing when he told the people, "The joy of the Lord is our strength."

Sabbath was designed to grow love in the sunlight of affirmation and to make sure that human worth was "filled to the brim" with the blessing of heaven.

The joy of blessing was demonstrated for me one day in an airline terminal. The plane was delayed, and people were trying to pass the time. A little boy was sitting with his father, and the wait was wearing on him. Suddenly his eyes lit up, and his face broke into a smile as he looked up at his dad and said, "Daddy, let's play the game."

Instinctively, his father knew what he wanted, and placing his son in front of him, he began by asking, "How much does your daddy love you?" With a mischievous smile, the little boy held his hands about two inches apart and looked back into his father's eyes, who responded, "Oh, no—your daddy loves you much more than that." The boy widened his hands to six inches. "No, much more than that." Ten inches—and the little boy continued to widen his hands.

The responses continued until the little boy's arms were stretched as far apart as they could possibly stretch. His hands were pointed at the opposite ends of the terminal. He was standing on his tiptoes trembling to reach out another centimeter and giggling with the anticipation of what would come next, for this was the moment of the game he loved most. His father sprang from the chair, grabbed him under his arms, tossed him into the air, and said, "Your daddy loves you *much* more than that!"

The little boy's laughter filled the terminal, and as he settled into his father's arms, he said, "Do it again, Daddy—do it again!"

When we experience our heavenly Father's Sabbath blessing, our heart rings with the laughter of love, and we long for it to come over us again and again.

"Do it again, Daddy!"

Sanctification: The Third Color of Love

Sanctification is the Hebrew word for marriage. It literally means, "Thou art one." On the sixth day God unites Adam and Eve in marriage, and they become one flesh. On the seventh day God unites humanity and divinity, and they become one spirit.

The final color of original love is sanctification. It means to be "set apart for a holy use." Combining the two meanings, we could infer that sanctification means, "dedicated to growing together in love." Jesus' prayer for His disciples is laced with marriage covenant language: "That they may be one, just as we are one. I in them and thou in Me, that they may be perfected in unity." John 17:22, 23.

This prayer is saturated with sanctification words and concepts. The importance of the concept of sanctification in scripture is demonstrated by the number of times that marriage and covenant language is used to describe our relationship with God.

Jesus applies sanctification language in two dimensions: praying for unity with God—and unity with man. Sanctifying love is designed to bring us into communion with God and into community with people. Through unity with God, we become His instruments to extend His love to one another.

As a Father, I know how much our children long to be with their parents. This was brought home to me in a vivid experience with my daughter, Tracy. She was three years old, and we had never left her with anyone but family. Mary Lou was asked to substitute teach for four weeks for one of the nursing professors who was to have surgery. Mary Lou would be away from Tracy for four hours each day.

We didn't think that this would be a problem. After all, we planned to leave her with Mrs. Wilson. Mrs. Wilson not only operated a daycare center during the week but also ran the kindergarten department at church. She was one of Tracy's favorite teachers.

When we sat down and explained the plan to Tracy, she seemed to handle it quite well until the night before Mary Lou's first day of teaching. That night, she began to exhibit a little anxiety as she was going to bed. The dialogue went like this:

"Mommy, please don't leave me."

"Tracy, I won't be gone very long, and you're going to stay with Mrs. Wilson."

"Mommy, please don't leave me."

"Tracy, I won't be gone long. I'll be back to get you right after lunch."

The morning came. I awakened Tracy, and her first question was, "Where is Mommy?" When I told her she was teaching, she said, "Oh, Daddy, please don't leave me."

I avoided any response and took her to eat breakfast. After the ordeal of a father attempting to put long hair into ponytails, which came close to reducing both of us to tears, we were finally ready to leave.

I took Tracy out to the car, and she whimpered, "Please don't leave me." We backed out of the driveway and started down the hill, and she whined, "I don't want to go to Mrs. Wilson's." As we approached the bottom of the hill, she asked, "Daddy, could I go to your office today and play in the corner—I'll be real quiet."

I explained that I didn't have office time today—that I had to go to meetings. She cried as we turned toward Mrs. Wilson's. I pulled up in front of the doors to the day care and walked her inside. Instead of the exuberance she normally displayed when she met Mrs. Wilson at church, she was reserved and clingy.

I finally got her to sit down by the toybox, and Mrs. Wilson said to me, "Go ahead and get her playing, and then you can just slip out." Tracy played anxiously for a while and then settled into playing with her favorite doll. When she was absorbed, I left for the door. Suddenly, Tracy realized that I was almost gone, and terror filled her face as she shrieked, "Daddy, please don't leave me!"

I stepped out through the sliding glass door and slid it closed as she ran after me, crying, "Daddy, please don't leave me!" As I got into the car, I realized that I had parked facing those sliding glass doors. I placed the key into the ignition and looked up to see the face of my daughter pressed against the glass door, tears streaming down, and her mouth shaping the words, "Please don't leave me, Daddy. Please don't leave me."

I started the car, backed out the driveway, and made it about a block before I turned around and went back to pick her up. The unifying instinct of Sabbath was too strong. *We must be together.* She rushed into my arms, and I wiped away her tears. We were one—and life was again as God had planned it.

The essence of sanctification is God's assurance that "I will never leave you nor forsake you."

3

The Primary Colors of Sin

PERFECT LOVE IN A PERFECT PLACE, celebrated each Sabbath—this was Paradise. Adam and Eve ate from the Tree of Life and reveled in the day of love. Everything in the Garden was for their enjoyment, with one exception—the Tree of Knowledge of Good and Evil. God had gifted them with freedom of choice that was so far-reaching that they could give themselves and their world to the devil.

Love and freedom are twin principles of the Garden. To remind them of love, God created Sabbath. To ensure freedom, He empowered them with choice. The power of choice is central to true love. For true love is never forced. It can only be given.

In the center of the Garden stood two trees symbolic of two ways of life. The Tree of Life was God's invitation to follow Him. The Tree of Knowledge of Good and Evil represents the alternative—to live independently, determining right and wrong from your perspective—in short, to be your own God.

The consequences of following either of these two alternatives are vastly different, because the two philosophies stand in direct opposition. Follow God and live—or leave God and die.

Goodness abounds, and Adam and Eve are invited to taste and see that the Lord is good. The way God introduces them to choice is instructive. While evil is available, it is circumscribed to one tree in the center of the Garden. Goodness is unlimited, and evil is limited. God will not allow Satan to roam throughout the Garden, mixing good with evil.

God will keep evil from you, but He will not keep you from evil. He will not allow it to grasp you, nor will He keep you from grasping it. God does confine the devil's freedom, but not yours. If He did not confine the devil, violence, calamity, and disasters would destroy all humanity.

One day Eve noticed the beauty of the Tree of Knowledge of Good and Evil and walked closer to observe its fruit. To her amazement, the encounter was enchanting. For the first time she had heard another voice and met another being.

The creature whispered another worldview and painted the vision of human potential. "You can become like God," was the promise. Just take the fruit and see that "You will not die—you'll really live!"

This other worldview doesn't look like death. There is no skull-and-crossbones; there are no scary figures of violence hanging from the tree. Instead, enticing fruit and a seductive being is in alluring disguise. There is a sense of independence available through knowledge. Brilliant minds paint God out of the picture of life. Reason is ultimate. Humans take center stage, and God is the source of limitation. There are slogans and promises that speak of human potential and power. The fruit doesn't look like poison. The aromas are sumptuous, the sights scintillating, and the creature friendly.

For the first time, Eve lets go of the Father's hand and reaches for the forbidden fruit. Heaven gasps and the serpent smiles as the perfect Garden is scarred.

Our world will never be the same. This is the moment of "Original Sin." Eve passes the fruit to Adam, and sin is compounded.

This is the moment that our world was introduced to pain, suffering, and death. Christians have codified the moment in the doctrine of original sin. I have been taught this doctrine from kindergarten on through to divinity school. It is important that we understand our sin problem. But it is even more important that we understand God's love solution. For in order to have original sin, there must be original love.

In our effort to understand our human problems, we have focused on original sin. However, Jesus spent little time during His ministry on earth defining sin. He spent most of His time demonstrating love.

In a private encounter with a sin-focused Pharisee, Nicodemus, Jesus whispered, "God so loved the world that He sent me . . . not to condemn it but to save it." He was explaining the perspective that Nicodemus would receive if he allowed God to recreate life in him. Jesus was inviting Nicodemus to be reborn in love and to allow God to reshape his soul through the power of the Spirit.

When a sin-focused scribe asked Jesus to summarize the commandments, His answer was saturated with love commands.

When Jesus found the Sabbath strangled by regulations, He asserted His authority to return it to original love, saying "The Sabbath was made for man and not man for the Sabbath. So the Son of Man is Lord even of the Sabbath."

He chose a Sabbath worship service in which to declare His mission: "He has sent Me to proclaim release to the captives and recovery of sight to the blind, to set free those who are downtrodden, to proclaim the favorable year of the Lord."

The only new commandment that Jesus gave was: "Love one another as I have loved you."

Perhaps if we followed the example of Jesus and spent more time defining love, we would discover the antidote for original sin. To focus on original sin without defining original love is to miss the most powerful, life-changing lesson of creation. Yes, original sin occurred, but thank God, original love came first!

God is love in person, the Sabbath is love in time, and the Church is love in place. God chose love as His self-defining term, because love is always relationship. He created a garden of love and formed creatures of choice, that love might reach new heights through freedom. As the final act of creation, God chose to stop all of His work and establish the Sabbath, a dedicated time in which love was to be experienced through rest, blessing, and sanctification. Because love requires time, it cannot be rushed. And in this day, He came to the Garden to grow the fruit of love.

When Adam and Eve chose to reach for another fruit and shattered their relationship with God, the Garden was lost, and we were left with a fallen world. But God would not allow His dream for love to be completely shattered. He would leave humans with a promise that He would return to save them and a hope that the Garden would one day be restored. He would leave reminders of love in this fallen world. Marriage would remain in their world to call couples to the commitment of love and to procreate children and experience family. Sabbath would remain in their week to call them back to God, so that together they might recreate original love.

Each Sabbath, God walks in our earth, ready to spend time with us that we may return to love—and live. Spending time with God is the way to imbed love in your life and overcome evil with good. Sabbath remains like the Tree of Life in a forest of "the knowledge of good and evil." It's time to stop looking at the forest and linger under the tree. The Father awaits you there and will guide you safely home.

The Primary Colors of Sin

The Garden was God's original plan for a life of love, but it didn't last. At the moment of original sin, the Garden becomes a jungle. Sin is no longer confined to one tree—it spreads like cancer across Paradise. Systematically, it begins to attack the first six days of creation with pain, suffering, and death. The earth shudders as the pristine soil loses its capacity to produce only good plants and is made ready by sin to produce weeds that will attack the flowers. The first rose petal falls.

Angels watch in horror as sin takes control of the surroundings. Slowly, everything from the first six days of creation is changed. But sin saves its most vicious attack for the seventh day. Genesis 3 records the impact:

"Then the eyes of both of them were opened, and they knew that they were naked; and they sewed fig leaves together and made themselves a covering.

"And they heard the sound of the Lord God walking in the garden in the cool of the day; the husband and wife hid themselves from the presence of the Lord God among the trees of the garden.

"Then the Lord God called to the man, and said to him, 'Where are you?'

"And Adam said, 'I heard the sound of You walking in the garden, and I was afraid, because I was naked; so I hid myself.'

"And He said, 'Who told you that you were naked? Have you eaten from the tree which I commanded you not to eat?'

"And the man said, 'The woman that you gave to be with me, she gave me fruit from the tree and I ate.'

"And the Lord God said to the woman, 'What is this you have done?' And the woman said, 'The serpent deceived me, and I ate.'"

What are the primary colors of sin? I find three: fear, shame, and blame. Each attacks one of the primary colors of love. Notice how sin attacks love as it shows its true colors.

FEAR attacks REST. Adam and Eve hide.

SHAME attacks BLESSING. They sense their own nakedness, feel worthless, and seek to cover up.

BLAME attacks SANTIFICATION. They turn on one another.

Even today, the original sin-attack has its damaging affect on our world in the twenty-first century. We live in a world in which disease and death are the norm. Thankfully, God has a cure! Original love serves as an antidote to sin. The healing properties of rest, blessing, and sanctification will cure the diseases of fear, shame, and blame.

Spiritual Lift and Drag

I believe that there is a "spiritual lift" and a "spiritual drag" in our lives. Sabbath is the God-designed force to provide "spiritual lift," so that we might "soar like the eagles" in experiencing original love. Sin is the force that drags us down spiritually, pulling us to live by the consequences of original sin in a wingless world.   This is illustrated in the diagram below:

Fear: The First Color of Sin

Fear robs us of rest. It breeds anxiety, worry, and overwork. It takes away our ability to rest by convincing us to hide from the Father. It convinces us that there is no goodness in the world and that the Father's primary goal is to punish us. Fear says, "The world is dangerous, and unless you hide you will not survive."

In his book *Sabbath* (pages 40 and 42), Wayne Muller explains this dynamic: "If we believe life is fundamentally good, we will seek out rest as a taste of that goodness. If we believe life is fundamentally bad or flawed, we will be reluctant to quiet ourselves, afraid of meeting the darkness…afraid of what we will find there. We will avoid the stillness at all cost, keeping ourselves busy not so much to accomplish but to avoid the terrors and dangers of emptiness." Pages 40, 42.

This dynamic sets the stage for turning work into toil. In God's original plan, Adam was given the privilege of meaningful work. "Be fruitful and multiply, and fill the earth, and subdue it, and rule over every living thing that moves on the earth." He was invited to join with God to fulfill the dream—in short, to populate the earth and govern its inhabitants. One of the curses of sin on the earth was turning the pleasant task of working with God to make the Garden thrive into toiling alone, fighting the weeds in order to grow enough food to survive.

Working to create goodness is the goal of God and man. One of the most practical lessons of creation for an overworked world is to understand the way God worked. There is a pattern: As the day ends, He inspects His work and declares it good. Wouldn't it be wonderful to be able to end your day by stepping back and reviewing your work and feeling so satisfied that you could say it is good? Sin has largely deprived us of time to review our work. We hardly have time to enjoy a job well done because of the need to produce more in order to ensure our value.

Sin has taken the divine rhythm out of work and thereby turned it into toil. Therefore, Jesus said, "Come unto me all you who labor to exhaustion [toil], and I will give you rest."

The underlying cause of fear is the sense that you're lost and that no matter how hard you try to find your way out of life's problems, you will ultimately fail. This fear of failure creates restlessness. And this is why we need Sabbath rest. "Perfect love casts out fear." Love conquers the darkest fear of all—fear of death! It assures us that all of our efforts will result in victory with Christ. We can "fight the good fight of faith" even when we are faced with the forces of evil.

Yes, life is a battle between the forces of good and evil, and we are the battleground. The question is, "What is our strategy for victory?" Will we fight for ourselves and make this a human war, or will we rest, allowing God to fight for us and make this a "holy war"?

The arming of the Spirit is where the fight is won or lost. Rest alone will bring victory and peace. Scripture records the battle cries of the "Holy Warriors":

Moses: "The Lord will fight for you while you keep silent."

Joshua: "The Lord your God gives you rest, and will give you this land."

Gideon: "Arise, for the Lord has given the camp of Midian into your hands."

Ruth: "Shall I not seek rest for you."

David: "The battle is the Lord's."

Jehoshaphat: "Go out and face them; God will fight for you."

When we put our trust in the Lord to provide for all our needs in this life and the life to come, we experience Sabbath rest. This is not a natural or easy journey. Just ask Abraham. He would hear the promise at age 75, realize it at 100, and memorialize it at 120 on Mount Moriah. We will relive this journey with him in the next chapter.

Shame: The Second Color of Sin

The moment that Adam and Eve sinned, they became self-conscious and ashamed. They had always been naked, but they had never been ashamed. Genesis 2:25 says, "And the man and his wife were both naked and were not ashamed.

Till this moment, their nakedness had been a comfortable part of their lives in the Garden. Shrouded by a garment of light, the natural beauty of their perfect bodies had enhanced their worth. But now the glow of love is gone, and for the first time they focus on their nakedness. Leaf after leaf is stripped from the fig trees; other plants and vines are harvested to fashion crude needles and thread. The garden is strewn with fragments of uprooted plants and torn leaves. Shame transforms Adam and Eve from caretakers to consumers. They turn on nature to find a way to cover their shame. They manufacture an external covering for an internal problem, and the same symptoms still prevail.

Their sexuality, designed to enable them to draw closer to God in procreation and to increase their worth through delivering life, becomes a source of embarrassment. God never intended that we would be ashamed of our bodies—sin distorted sexuality. God never pointed out their nakedness.

Adam confesses that he hid in fear because they realized they were naked. God asked, "Who told you that you were naked? Have you eaten from the tree that I commanded you not to eat?" Adam chooses to answer the tree question, avoiding the knowledge question. We can only assume that the knowledge either came from their own awareness courtesy of the serpent in the other tree. The point is, if you do not feel bad about yourself as a natural consequence of your decision to leave God, the devil will see to it that he shames you. You can count on it—the snake will put you down and keep you down. Sin always attacks worth!

The answer to shame is neither clothing nor cosmetics. The answer is: Blessing. The Sabbath blessing stands in stark contrast as the antidote to shame: "They looked to Him and were radiant, and their faces shall never be ashamed." Psalm 34:5.

This is why it is so important to receive the Sabbath blessing in your life daily, weekly, and eternally. In this worth-draining world, I meet so many people who need to know that they have a heavenly Father who loves them.

Most of these people have never fully experienced love from their earthly father, and it has caused them to doubt the existence of a loving heavenly Father. If this is true for you, you are not alone.

Martin Luther's relationship with his own father was strained. His dad wanted him to be a lawyer, and when Martin chose the priesthood, his father told him that he would never be a success. This lack of affirmation from his earthly father affected Luther's ability to pray the beginning of the Lord's prayer: "Our Father." Because coming into the presence of his earthly father was so demeaning, it affected his ability to think of God as a loving Father.

This is true today for people who have been put down, abandoned, or abused by an earthly father. I would call on every father who reads this book to follow the example of God and instill worth by blessing your children each Sabbath. In the practice section on "Experiencing Sabbath Blessing," we will explain how to give a blessing. In the story of Jacob and Leah, you will experience the power of the blessing. Their journey to blessing will change your life and may even change your name.

Blame: The Third Color of Sin

Original sin caused Adam and Eve to run from God and turn on each other. Separation replaced unity. There is nothing more wrenching than hearts broken apart by sin.

When a heartbroken God asks His estranged children to explain their breakup, they resort to blame. The irony of blame is that it can only defend the breaking but it can never mend the break. When blame continues, it will only deepen the hurt and drive us into bitterness. Seductively, the serpent continues slowly constricting our spirit with coils of blame and leads us to isolation in a prison of self-pity filled with thoughts of revenge.

Blame is a symptom of separation. It was the first tactic that Adam and Eve used when God asked, "Have you eaten from the tree which I commanded you not to eat? And the man said, 'the woman that You gave to be my wife, she gave me the fruit of the tree and I ate it.'"

First, we break up with God and then with each other. In the backwash of his separation from God, Adam breaks with Eve. Adam points the finger of blame at both of them, "*You* gave her to me, and *she* gave me the fruit." In other words, "It's really not my fault, God."

The earth separates along fault lines, and our physical foundations are shaken with earthquakes. When we find fault with one another, we experience separation, with "blame quakes." They shake the foundation of love, and cracks appear in our relationships. The more we resort to blame, the wider the breaks become. But it takes two to play the blame game, and Eve joins the blame party.

"Then the Lord said to the woman, 'What is this you have done?' And the woman said, 'The serpent deceived me, and I ate.'"

Eve is the original "victim." She alleges that her actions were beyond her control and that the forces of evil were so great that she was powerless to resist—so blame the snake. One of the most accepted defenses of our time is that my wrong is beyond my control. I am a victim of poor parenting, social injustice, or genetic predisposition. In short, "the devil made me do it." We have refined this defense to the point that it exonerates the victim.

The rules of choice demand that God separate Himself from Adam and Eve. His children must leave the Garden of life and step into the jungle of death. The curse of death must fall as the rule of the serpent begins. But even at this moment, at the pronouncement of their self-chosen sentence, God promises to come to free them from death. He will not allow their punishment to have eternal consequences. They can be freed from death, because He will reinstate the opportunity to choose life.

God's words are found in Genesis 3:14-24. As you read them, notice that while He must pass judgment upon Adam and Eve, He does not reprimand them for blaming Him. Nor does He mix their sentence of separation with a guilt trip of blame. How easy it would have been for God to turn the blame on them. He had the facts. He had caught them naked. They had blown a perfect life opportunity! They were an easy target for blame. But love disciplines for healing, not for revenge.

God is hard on the problem of sin, but soft on the sinners. He curses the serpent and the ground but not Adam or Eve. His justice is delivered in love as He sends them from the garden. He fashions new clothes to cover their bodies and gives them a promise to warm their spirits.

Even though they have chosen to leave God, He will never leave them. That is the message of sanctifying love in a world of sin. From this moment on, Sabbath will be an invitation to man to return to unity with God. The power of sanctification will be used to reunite humans to Him through forgiveness, to meet with Him in a place called a sanctuary and to allow Him to regrow a community of love, and once again be one.

The power of sanctification to restore broken relationships and rebuild family is profoundly illustrated in the life of Joseph. He is the patriarch whose life was shattered by the power of blame and put back together by the power of sanctification. Joseph experienced brokeness and blame:

◆ Grew up in a dysfunctional family.

◆ Pampered by his father; despised by his brothers.

◆ A victim of family violence.

◆ Sold into slavery by his brothers.

◆ Exiled to a foreign land.

◆ Subject to racial segregation.

◆ Sexually harassed by his master's wife.

◆ Falsely accused of rape.

◆ Sentenced to jail because of racial prejudice.

◆ Languished in jail for a crime he did not commit.

If Joseph had chosen the path of blame, he could have become a very vengeful person. But God would sanctify his life, heal his brokenness, and bring him Sabbath. Joseph's journey to sanctification is a testimony to the power of Sabbath love in a world of sin. I believe his story can take the broken pieces of your life and turn them into peace!

4

How to Experience Original Love

AFTER DISCOVERING THE PRIMARY COLORS of love, Mary Lou and I embarked on a journey to experience original love each Sabbath. It started with comb ing scripture to find practical ways through which God had integrated the Sabbath into the experience of Bible personalities. Next, we prayed that God would give us creative minds as we began to explore how to practice these ways each week. Gradually, the Sabbath grew from being just a part of the creation story, to becoming a prized family day. We deliberately planned ways to experience rest, blessing, and sanctification. The more we practiced these principles, the more God seemed to unfold new ideas—it was as if He joined us in recreating the Sabbath.

The Principle of Advanced Planning

A fundamental assumption of creationism is advanced planning. We believe that the order and beauty of the universe are the result of advanced planning on the part of a divine being who created our world. His planning makes it possible for the disciplines of science to emerge. If the physical laws of our world were not predictable, scientists would be unable to send astronauts into space or create drugs to cure disease. The more you inspect God's work, the more you respect His attention to detail.

Mary Lou and I began to realize that when it came to the Sabbath, we were acting more like evolutionists than creationists. Let me explain! If the Sabbath was conceived by God as the day for love, and if He imbued it with the primary colors of love, then it only stands to reason that we will receive its fullest blessings of love as we plan in advance for its arrival.

We realized that we were not doing any advance planning of our Sabbaths such as the Lord did in creating His day. In fact, we were quite passive, since we were depending on others to make the Sabbath meaningful for us. Our Sabbath experience was dependent on the teacher's lesson or the preacher's sermon. When the lesson and sermon were inspiring, our Sabbath was great, but when they were not, our Sabbath experience was diminished. We were like an evolutionist waiting for a "holy accident" to happen. Sometimes it occurred, and we were blessed. But when it didn't, we were disappointed. The seventh day of creation was not a "holy accident." God did not wait to see what might happen on Sabbath. Rather, He carefully planned it in advance so that it would be a perfect day. He planned His perfect day around Rest, Blessing and Sanctification.

We determined to experiment with this idea of advanced planning and therefore decided to plan a month of Sabbaths in advance. We created a Sabbath Planning Worksheet and began our planning (a sample worksheet is at the end of this chapter). This resulted in four of the most meaningful Sabbaths we have ever experienced!

Thus we adopted advanced planning as a regular part of our Sabbath preparation. It became a team project, with each member of our family participating. We noticed that our planning for Sabbaths in advance created positive anticipation for the Sabbath's arrival. Sabbath became a true delight.

If you desire to experience Sabbath delight, why not give advanced planning a try. Make it a part of your Sabbath practice to take time to plan the next four Sabbaths. We believe that if you do, you will find that you will begin to experience the exquisite joy of Sabbath in your life.

One family who attended our Sabbath seminar and adopted the practice of advanced planning enjoyed their four planned Sabbaths so much that they referred to advanced planning as the process for creating "Super Sabbaths." God did not design Sabbath as a blind date with divinity but as a planned invitation to spiritual delight.

The word God chose to define Himself is *love*. The pinnacle of creation is the seventh day, because it is the day for love. God is love in person. The Sabbath is love in time. God calls His fallen children to abide in Him and remember the Sabbath. The Sabbath is the signature day of creation, because it contains the principles of original love.

Recreating the Sabbath

History tells us that humans tend to destroy the Sabbath by distorting its message of love. When Jesus came to save the world, He found that humans had taken possession of His day. The Sabbath had been distorted from being a day for love to being a day for law. Legalism had drained the delight from His creation. But instead of abandoning the day, Jesus set out to restore it, despite the protests of the lawyers. It was His commitment to the Sabbath as a day for love that caused such great conflict with the Pharisees. They claimed that their interpretation of the day was from God, and He claimed it was from the devil. It was His claim to be Lord of the Sabbath and His actions of love that caused them to determine to take His life.

Calvary forever stands as Jesus' response to original sin. The twin towers of love in scripture are Calvary's cross and creation's Sabbath. Redemption defines love in an imperfect world, and Sabbath defines love in a perfect world. Redemption reveals the means to life, and Sabbath reveals the meaning of life. Through original love, God redeemed the people and restored the day. He would not allow sin to determine the destiny of His people or of His day.

The perversion that legalism brought to the Sabbath caused people to see God as being against them. This resulted in a negative approach to a positive day. Their questions focused on what they could or could not do on the Sabbath. Human religious leaders trying to control the people in the name of God caused the Sabbath to lose its blessing.

The Pharisees focused on behavior. Jesus focused on goodness.

They became experts in viewing the Sabbath through the reverse end of the telescope, causing the three great principles of love to be minimized. Instead of asking what one *could* do to experience Rest, Blessing, and Sanctification, they focused on what should *not* be done. They created endless lists of prohibitions that focused people on duty and deprived them of delight. Jesus emphasized doing good on the Sabbath, while the Pharisees emphasized avoiding evil.

Finally, the Pharisees implied that ceasing activity was to align oneself with God. They took their mandate from just one dimension of the meaning of rest (to cease). They specialized in teaching people what to stop doing, serving in the role of "stop cops." Their view of the Sabbath implied that God was all about restriction of life and that His day was about ceasing to live—instead of learning to live. Out of a day of love, they created a day simply to endure. We must always realize that God is ever a God of action. He is never passive and does not take delight in exacting rules of restriction on His children. Love is a verb, and Sabbath is the day of love's expression in our lives.

The first focus of Sabbath planning is to ask, "What can I do to practice rest, blessing, and sanctification?" By contrast, the first focus of legalism is to ask, "Is it permissible to do_____on the Sabbath?" The first question is motivated by a desire to maximize the principle of love. The second is based on avoiding Sabbath transgression. One question views the Sabbath as love and freedom, the other as law and restriction. **To maximize the Sabbath is to experience original love.**

If God is love, then every time He encounters human beings, He leaves the imprint of love in some dimension of their experience. In the creation story, He closes with the establishment of the seventh day and original love.

When Jesus comes to this earth to live as a human being, He lived love. When He left the earth and commanded the creation of the church, He left behind the Holy Spirit, which teaches love.

This consistent love instruction is just a part of the Spirit's coming to us, and as He comes, He keeps revealing new dimensions of His love to enrich our lives.

The Menorah—A Symbol of the Sabbath

Once Mary lou and I built our Sabbaths around experiencing Rest, Blessing, and Sanctification, we found that practicing these principles could give greater joy to life throughout the week. Sabbath became the power source for daily living. Gradually, it expanded far beyond a worship experience—all the way to a lifestyle. This is the true purpose of Sabbath. It should have a spiritual impact on all our transactions in life. God intended it to be day that would make all other days meaningful.

The Jewish people understood this and symbolized it in the *menorah*— a seven-branched candelabra that represented the days of creation. The candle representing the Sabbath is placed in the center of the candelabra, with three days of the week on either side. The first three days of the week (Sunday through Tuesday) we are to live in the memory of Sabbath, and the last three days of the week (Wednesday through Friday), we live in the anticipation of and preparation for the arrival of Sabbath. The Sabbath infuses love into every day.

God's plan was to create a perfect garden where humans could experience perfect love. Unfortunately, humans spoiled His plan by choosing original sin. But God would not give up. He would seek to rescue His fallen world through establishing a chosen people. He built their identity and culture around the Sabbath and showed them the power of original love. Through them, He would seek to reach the world with the message of a God of love.

It occurred to me that the lives of the patriarchs were case studies in the power of Sabbath in a fallen world. I began to study their lives to learn what they could teach us about how to live the Sabbath right here, right now.

Abraham and Sarah's journey to Rest.

Jacob and Leah's journey to Blessing.

Joseph and Aseneth's journey to Sanctification.

For the remainder of this book, we will consider each of their life journeys and unpack how they came to experience the power of original love. Though this study, God will impress you with His agenda for your life, and I believe you will be empowered to build your own legacy of love.

Sabbath Plans

Sabbath Concepts I Want to Experience	1st Sabbath Date _____	2nd Sabbath Date _____	3rd Sabbath Date _____	4th Sabbath Date _____
ADVANCED PLANNING What I can do to prepare for Sabbath each day of the week				
REST What I can do to stop, relax, and get to know God				
BLESSING What I can do to sense God's favor and rejoice in His love for me				
SANCTIFY What I can do to draw close to God, forgive others, and grow love				

Experiencing Sabbath Advance Planning

OUR FAMILY IDEAS, PRESENTED IN the "Experiencing Sabbath in . . . Advanced Planning, Rest, Blessing, and Sanctification" sections in this book are shared as a means of "jumpstarting" your creativity in these areas. These ideas have our family stamp on them. It is important for you to personalize them to your family, creating your own family stamp. What follows is only a sampling of the ideas our family has practiced over many years. Other ideas and activities, such as for experiencing the Sabbath in nature, God's second book— or on rainy Sabbaths, may be found on our website: *originalove.com.*

The goal of the practical applications for Advance Planning, Rest, Blessing and Sanctification is to establish positive spiritual memories and traditions of eternal significance. In our planning, we make a conscious effort to touch all the senses for the Lord.

ADVANCE PLANNING: To recognize that God planned the creation of the Sabbath in advance—and that we can do no less.

Examples of ways to plan in advance for Sabbath:

1. We plan four Sabbaths in advance. Usually, we do our planning

on Sunday morning in conjunction with our weekly family calendar coordination. After sharing our ideas as a family, we made our weekly list (see below). An example of our planning sheet appears just before this section.

2. Weekly list: On a weekly calendar, each of the family members decided what they would do each day of the week to get ready for the Sabbath (i.e.: buy picnic items; do housecleaning chores, prepare clothing; buy the Sabbath candles; buy the Sabbath surprises (see the "Experiencing Sabbath Rest" section); buy in advance any tickets to museums, parks, or nature centers or other items needed for Sabbath afternoon activity; get new items for the Sabbath bag, items for the Sabbath centerpiece, and so on.

3. Prepare tithes and offerings in advance of Sabbath. Following Paul's admonition to "set aside your offerings on the first day of the week, we desired to establish the understanding with our children that everything belongs to the Lord and that in gratitude, we give His tithes and our offerings. Our family time on Sunday morning worked best for us. Children especially like to have their offering all ready in their purse, "church pants" pocket, or wallet —eagerly waiting for the offering plate.

4. Practice church at home. This was not only fun but a wonderful teaching opportunity when the children were younger. We would set up the chairs, line up the teddy bears and stuffed animals, sing with our "grown up songbooks," and kneel quietly for prayer, remembering to pray for the pastor(s). We also took turns "playing preacher" and learned to listen quietly until he/she was finished. We spent time talking about this special time of reverent celebration called church.

5. Prepare for the church service. We would call the church office to obtain the list of songs to be sung on Sabbath and practice them at home. Many times we would use our family worships to read about these songs from a book on the history of hymns that we have. This served two purposes: Because the kids were familiar with the song, they could sing along—and it had more meaning if they identified with its history.

6. Select a special place to watch the sun setting on Friday evening to welcome the Sabbath with song and prayer. Here is where the

Weekly List assisted us in being ready to welcome the Sabbath as a beloved guest!

7. When the pastor had a series of sermons on a Bible character, we used this opportunity to read age-appropriate books at our family worships during the week. Other family worship ideas may be found on our Web site: *originalove.com.*

The Journey to Rest

5

Restless in Ur

IMAGINE THAT YOU HAVE JOINED an archaeological dig at the ancient city of Shechem and suddenly scrolls are found, buried near the roots of a old oak tree. Excitement fills the air as scholars decipher the contents and report that this is the journal of the patriarch Abraham. The scroll is scanned and computer-translated. Drafts of the script are distributed. And you begin to read these words of the ancient patriarch . . .

Anxiety plagues my life! Not the anxiety of uncertainty, but rather that born of certainty. I know the certainty of a life without children in Ur. Children are prized in our culture. And a son is the most prized. Through a son, you can multiply your tribe, your workforce, and therefore your wealth. Through a son, you ensure that you will be cared for in old age. Through a son, you continue your family legacy.

To get married and fail to have children is a disgrace. I have watched this social stigma crush the joy out of the lives of many otherwise happy couples. I have seen the acceptable and expected solution of a second marriage—the quest for a fertile mate—rip holes in the fabric of a home, and I could not accept this as our future. I loved Sarai, and it wounded us both to have her labeled barren—categorized by society and rejected by other women as judged by God.

The pressure of being a barren couple had been mounting for years. We had sought medical help without results. I had watched my beautiful bride's optimism slowly fade to fatalism. We were approaching the point of desperation It seemed that everywhere we turned, we were confronted by the same question: "Are you ever going to have children?" It became an obsession. We found ourselves avoiding social gatherings, trapped by our own anxiety over the certainty of where the conversation would focus. It would inevitably lead to the subject of children.

The complicating factor was our age. Long past youth and the prime childbearing years, we were staring into the face of a biological impossibility. The thought of having many children had long since been abandoned. I now wanted just one—a son to keep my name alive.

Have you ever been restless in Ur?

I went to bed but could not sleep. I tossed and turned as my mind wrestled with my anxious spirit. Finally, I slipped out of bed and climbed the stairs to the rooftop. It was a stunning night. The cool breeze and the starlit sky seemed to draw me toward heaven. I walked and talked with God, interceding for Sarai, pleading for a son.

Have you ever been restless in Ur?

It shouldn't happen—Ur is a fabulous place to live. I was so fortunate to have been raised there. It holds every opportunity for happiness—wealth, education, and culture. It is the land of opportunity and has been good to our family. But I was restless because amid all that I had, I did not have peace. I shared my emptiness with God. I thought that the only thing missing was a child. A son would make Ur complete. I had no idea how wrong I was.

The last thing I expected was the next thing that took place. God spoke to me out of the darkness of the night! I heard His voice!

"Go forth from your country,
And from your relatives

And from your father's house,

To the land which I will show you;

And I will make you a great nation.

And I will bless you,

And make your name great;

So you shall be a blessing."

God's voice faded, and I was alone. As I rehearsed the promise, rest began to fill my heart with a sense of peace. First, I went to the study and copied the words on this piece of parchment. And then I woke Sarai and told her the story. I will never forget how she took the parchment in her hands and read it several times, as if absorbing every ounce of hope the promise contained. Like travelers on the desert in search of water, this was our oasis in the nightmare of barren living.

We were drawn to the words "I will make you a great nation." This was far beyond our wildest dreams! One child—maybe two—but never a nation!

Have you ever been restless in Ur?

Have you stopped dreaming because hope was crushed? Have circumstances drained vitality from your spirit and replaced enthusiasm with apathy? Have you been tempted to lower your sights from greatness?

The next morning I shared the promise with Dad. His response was equally unexpected. He said, "Abram, you must go for yourself. Pursue God's vision for you. Don't allow Ur to mold you. I will go with you."

Can you imagine it? Here is an old man who has completed his life's work and now deserves to relax and enjoy the benefits of his labor—the honor of his community and the care of his family. That is what everyone else does as they travel the road of retirement. But not Dad! When he heard of God's promise, he put all that he had on the line. He didn't just offer to bless me and send me away. He offered to go with me and live the adventure. He was my encourager.

Two things enabled me to leave Ur. My heavenly Father's vision—and my earthly father's encouragement. Sarai and I took the leap of faith, and together with Lot began our journey to the promised land. It was an adventure of a lifetime!

Have you ever risked everything for God?

Most of the time we are too cautious with God. We allow Him only limited access to our lives. Occasionally our spiritual imagination is stirred by the sense that God is calling us to greatness. We are inspired by the thought. But all too often we turn back from the leap of faith to take a baby step on a predictable road of our own choosing. The limits of our lives are set by the limits of our faith. God never limits us—we limit ourselves!

We began our journey without a map and without a compass. Some would call it presumption, but when you have heard God's call, that is enough. Our caravan was a procession of praise. We shared our story at every campsite and village. The people were amazed, and they always asked the same questions:

"God spoke to you?"

"You're going to start a new nation?"

"Where do you plan to settle?"

"How are you going to survive?"

"Don't you think this is putting your family at risk?"

Faith is never completely rational, or it would become simply knowledge. Faith intersects reason, but goes far beyond to stretch you to the impossible. God stands at the border of the possible and bids you to walk with Him into the promised land. Faith is most convincing when intelligent, rational people embrace it as the final reality and break the limits of human logic and the boundaries of scientific knowledge. There is only one dimension of knowledge that is necessary to begin the journey—and that is to know that it is God who is calling.

Have you ever risked everything to follow Him?

Are you still restless in Ur?

Pray and listen—and you will hear your promise and begin your journey to rest.

6

The Halfway Hazard— Stuck in Haran

WE WERE HALFWAY to the promised land when Dad became ill. He assured us that all he needed was a few days of rest, and he would be ready to go again. We stopped in Haran—a famous city on the trade route that had the most modern medical facilities. A few days of rest and relaxation in Haran would be just what the doctor ordered.

Days turned to weeks as it became apparent that Dad would not have a swift recovery. We all settled down and took up residence in Haran. We became quite at home while waiting for Dad to recover.

Then the unexpected happened. Dad died! I felt so empty—this was the first great disappointment in our journey of faith. It seemed like a cruel joke to have to bury Dad halfway between Ur and the promised land. To deny an old man the chance to see the promised land after he had exercised such faith just didn't seem right.

I knew Dad was getting up in years, but I just wanted to get him to Canaan so he could see the promised land with his own eyes. That would have been enough. Why didn't God allow it? Why now? Why here?

Have you ever been stuck in Haran?

Everyone has a Haran—a place where death attacks the spirit and the soul goes numb. A place—a time in life—when the promise is intecepted by pain. When the power of sin is so shocking that faith is shaken by the cruel hand of circumstance.

Have you ever been stuck in Haran?

Has your journey of faith been attacked by the loss of health, the death of a loved one, divorce, loss of a job, or unexpected failure? Have you experienced a time when the blows of sin knocked the breath of God from the lungs of your faith? These are the times when it is easy to abandon the journey to rest.

Have you ever been disappointed with God?

Have you ever needed a second call?

Time passed. After we buried Dad, I somehow lost my spiritual motivation. Faith drifted into apathy, and I began to speak less of the promise and more of Haran. I didn't feel like praying, and the promise hung unread on the wall. I began to bargain away its entitlements. And finally, the only one that seemed to matter was to have a son.

My thoughts raced with desperation as I paced beneath the midnight sky and mumbled pleadings for God to hear and give us just one piece of the promise—a child.

And then it happened.

God spoke the second time! The same promise that had ignited my faith in Ur was repeated, and the same assurances were affirmed. It was as if God were telling me that though circumstances had changed, He had not changed. "Abram, your earthly father is dead, but your heavenly Father is alive. Your expectations may not come to pass, but my promise will. The road that you imagine is smooth, but the reality of your world is rough. It's time to resume the journey."

Have you ever needed a second call?

It doesn't matter how dark your night is. When you hear God's voice again, suddenly it is the high noon of hope. I never listened so intently in my life, and when we finished talking, I lingered in the aura of His afterglow. My insecurities, anxieties, and fears were eclipsed by His presence, His promise, and His calling. My confusion was lifted like a vanishing fog. He breathed a second wind into my soul.

God's second call is your way out of being stuck in the ruts of life. God's prophecy ignites hope's flame, and you become fully alive.

If you are stuck in Haran, you need a second call. Good news! The heavenly Father never tires of calling His children—and I'm living proof.

I raced back to Sarai's side and woke her. The news was too good to keep until morning. She was skeptical at first, not sure that she wanted to risk another disappointment. She raised all the objections. She interrogated me—and why not? She had been disappointed once, and when you have been disappointed, it is only natural to be cautious the second time.

Have you ever had an encounter with God and somehow embraced the idea that after this, everything would be different—only to find that within a short time reality had encroached on revelation, and you were back to facing the same issues in your life? Failure discounts your faith, and harsh reality forces you to confronted the fact that you have not arrived—that instead you have only just begun.

The next morning I gathered the family, shared the story, and read the promise. I took this parchment from the wall and retraced every letter with fresh ink. Then I hung it on the door. Word of my experience and of the promised child spread throughout Haran.

A promise is a powerful thing. It enables you to hope, to dream, to rejoice. It reminds you that God's in charge—and that's so important. Reality tends to drain hope from your spirit. Dreams are compromised. Life is diminished.

If I have learned anything, it is that the aging of the body is inevitable, but the aging of the spirit is elective. You can have an aging body and an ageless spirit if you listen to the promise and rest in the Lord.

God's promises are like love vitamins of the spirit. The miracle of life is that your spiritual life can grow and thrive as your physical life declines. Death is only skin deep. Life, on the other hand, goes to the very core of the soul.

What *you* see is not reality. What *God* sees is.

Yet it's hard to see beyond the horizon of the present, and even when you do embrace God's view, others all around you go out of their way to argue that reason and reality simply make the promise impossible. You don't start a nation at the age of 75. The mother of a nation is not a woman who has never given birth and will shortly enter menopause.

Have you ever been stuck in Haran?

We left Haran. We invested all we had in God's promise. We were tempted to go back to Ur, to the old familiar way of living, but we were still powered by the promise. We had to get out of this spiritual no-man's land. And so do you, if you are ever stuck in Haran, halfway between the past and the future, lingering under gray skies and sleepless nights.

Listen for the promise. Claim it as your own. Rest in the Lord. Get out of Haran!

7

Grand Expectations

I DID NOT HAVE THE FAINTEST IDEA of the journey Sarai and I were about to take. My expectations and God's were daylight and darkness apart. It was only natural to expect that Sarai would get pregnant soon. After all, God had called us to move. It seemed logical to conclude that He must be ready to begin a nation, and that required children, and Sarai was my only wife.

Finally, time was running out. She was 65, and I was 75. God needed to act. The biological clock was ticking. My dad, Terah, had fathered all three of his sons by my age, and most men begin their families in their early 30s. There was no time to waste.

I have often wondered why God gave me the promise without any indication of how long it would take to fulfill it. If He had told me it would take 25 years, I don't know what I would have done. I have thought about it often, and sometimes I have thought it would have been so nice to know, to have a timetable. But on the other hand, time has a cruel way of controlling you, limiting you, reminding you that you are on a death march numbered by years.

Eternity does not live within the shackles of time. Why, if I had known that it would take 25 years, I may not have believed the promise in the first place! My tendency would have been to calculate the years and realize that Sarai would be 90 and I would be 100—and the impossibility of time would have certainly cast a fog over my faith.

I am just about positive I wouldn't have awakened Sarai that night to tell her that in 25 years God was going to give her a son. What kind of news would that have been? We humans want to know things that will come true tomorrow, not in 25 years, and who would be excited enough to wake his wife with the news that 25 years from now, you are going to have a baby. It would be almost cruel to ask a woman to believe that biology would be no barrier. To encourage Sarai to tell the community that in 25 years she was going to have a baby would set the stage for scorn and ridicule.

It was bad enough to tell everyone that at age 65 we were moving to create a nation. The most dramatic difference between God's reality and my expectation was that one word—*time.*

That's not an easy assignment. We humans don't think of an eternity. We're locked in time. Time is a human attempt to understand eternity. It holds you hostage in the kingdom of the temporal, and it keeps you locked out of the rest of the eternal.

Over the next 25 years, I would learn to wait on the Lord. My greatest continual companion of disbelief was the underlying anxiety born of the view that time was running out.

In my day, we only knew the seasons, the months, and the rising and setting of the sun. Time was marked by natural changes, by natural cycles.

You modern folks have created the artificial marking of time by clocks. You bear the handcuffs of time on your wrist. It intrudes on your life. From alarms to schedules, you are trapped in time.

You measure the value of each person by how much they produce in a period of time. You call it productivity. To show value, you complete more tasks in the same time. You speed up everything. You have stressed your lives.

On my journey, time has been my stressor, and eternity my comforter. I realize that time is a fact of life. But God is not confined by time. It is the prison from which you must escape to experience eternity. Sabbath is the secret. That is why God created it and why He encourages us to remember and keep it. Taking the time to "relax and know God" fills you with rest and peace. You are able to view your world from the timeless perspective of God's love, which casts out all fear. Without the Sabbath, we are confined to a life at hard labor, "doing time" in the prison of the temporal.

Rest is all about taking time out—a sabbatical. Within the sacred confines of Sabbath time, we once again return to the natural rhythm of the garden. The other six days of the week, we are driven by the world of the temporal. But Sabbath returns us to creation. As the setting of the sun marked the days, so with the setting of the sun on Friday evening we allow love to make time stand still, laying down all earth's demands and enjoying heaven's blessings. Once again the evening breeze stirs as the Father comes to be with His children. His call to a temporal world far from the garden is, "Come unto me all you who labor to exhaustion—and I will give you rest!" (See Matthew 11:28.)

8

Egypt

HAVE YOU EVER BEEN TO EGYPT?

Before you answer, let me explain. I am not talking about a physical trip to a geographic location. I am talking about a spiritual journey based on a mindset.

Have you ever been to Egypt?

The mind-set of Egypt is foreign to faith in God. In my day Egypt was a place where man was God. A place where the God of heaven was ignored and humanity was exalted. It was as ancient as the serpent's suggestion, "You shall be like God," and as modern as the teachings of New Age philosophy.

It's the mantra of self-achievement, first uttered in heaven's courts, then at Eden's tree, next at Babel's tower, and now in Pharaoh's courts. It is not a claim without substance, for the culture is dynamic, the economy is strong, the monuments are awesome. But the message is deadly: "Trust in yourself—you can become like God."

Have you ever been to Egypt?

Have you ever taken things into your own hands? Have you ever simply trusted in yourself and forgotten about God?

I have. I neglected a habit—a key to my life—that started when I first received the promise. It was the family altar. I built an altar when I first arrived in Canaan. It was the place where our family would go and worship and talk to God. Every morning, when I arose, I took the parchment and walked out to the altar and began my day with God.

The altar served many purposes in our home. It was a reminder that we were a chosen people with an eternal Father and a divine destiny. It called us to worship. It became a symbol of power and sacred presence. It became a place where we would retell the stories of God's leading. It became a witness to everyone who passed by that we were worshipers of Jehovah. It reminded us that God would provide for all our needs.

But I neglected it. One of the keys to the Sabbath is to practice its principles throughout the week. It is far too easy to worship at church but forget to worship at home. Time crushes God from our daily lives, and we fall prey to restlessness. How is it with you? Is Sabbath worship celebrated daily at your family altar?

Losing track of the family altar leads to acting on your own, informed only by your own perspective. The Promised Land let us down. There was no rain, and a famine swept the land. When it came to the famine, the logic was compelling, and the alternatives were few. Egypt was where we needed to go. Why bother God with the discussion? After all, if the solution is apparent, then action is the order of the day.

Our problems come in two sizes—human-sized and God-sized. A God-sized problem is Sarai's inability to have children. I can't do a thing about that. God's my only hope. That is something worth praying about.

But food—that's a human-sized problem. I know how to solve it. I need not occupy God with this issue. I need not seek His counsel.

Have you ever been to Egypt?

It's a trip that begins with simply taking your eyes off God. Whether this is prompted by breathtaking fruit on a forbidden tree—or by famine—it doesn't really matter. Distraction is the first step toward letting go of the Father's hand to wander alone in the devil's land. It sets the stage for a faith attack.

Unlike a heart attack, in a faith attack you feel no immediate pain. In fact, you may sense the exhilaration of independence and the ego adrenaline of grappling with a problem and finding what seems to be a solution. But sooner or later you realize you have strayed from God, and your human attempts to solve a problem have only made matters worse. You are tangled in Satan's web.

Have you ever been to Egypt?

As we neared Egypt, it suddenly dawned on me that I had another life-threatening problem: Sarai. She is beautiful, and Egyptians favor beautiful Chaldean women. Lot told me that it was not unusual for border guards to receive a promotion for finding beautiful women to be incorporated into Pharaoh's harem. The rewards were so great that if they found that the woman was married, they simply murdered her husband and took the wife.

I was facing the potential of treachery. I was walking into a death trap. This required some clever thinking. If the promise was to be realized, I had to stay alive. How could I outwit the Egyptians?

I finally came up with a plan that would save my skin. The hardest part was how to get out of this problem without telling a lie, and the solution seemed ingenious. I asked Sarai to say that I was her brother and not her husband. Clever. Technically true. She is my half sister.

I know what you're thinking, but if they're not smart enough to ask, I'm not dumb enough to tell. I shared the idea with Sarai, and she thought it was rather brilliant. I have to admit, I was pleased with myself.

Have you ever been to Egypt?

It's a land that engages you in games of human achievement, inviting you to explore your potential, free from the Father's hand. You let go—and nothing happens. You sense independence, freedom, self-confidence. You cross the border—a child of God in the land of sin. It happened to me.

At first it looked as if I were a genius. The scenario played out just as I had anticipated. The Egyptians accepted Sarai's explanation that I was her brother. They even treated us with special favor. We found food in abundance, a place to live, and life was good. But then, as unpredictably as an earthquake, as unexpectedly as lightning from a blue sky, everything started to unravel. The man of God's choosing has played the game of life alone.

Nothing excites the forces of evil more than a child of God straying from the Father's side.

It's Pharaoh's move, and he takes Sarai to his harem to be prepared as a wife. I was stunned by the turn of events and devastated by the reality that my clever plans had been turned against Sarai. It revealed the ugly truth of my self-centered thinking. I had no grounds to appeal for Sarai's return. I was trapped in a house of cards built on a half truth. I could not assert my marriage right.

It quickly became apparent that Pharaoh intended to marry her. The dowry began to arrive. First silver and gold, then livestock. I was instantly wealthy. You see, the wages of sin can look like success more often than failure. God does not rain down judgment upon you the minute you stray. In fact, He even allows the devil to bring you pleasure and reward.

In a few short days, my life changed from famine survivor to celebrity. Money, status, and power were mine for the taking. All I had to do was let the Egypt scenario run its course, and my life would be secured. All I had to give up was Sarai and the promise. Egypt's alternatives are seductive. First, you take things into your own hands, then you play the game of life with your own strategy, and finally the rewards of the immediate threaten the potential of the eternal.

Have you ever been to Egypt?

If I were looking for material security, then this was the right solution. Sarai would never have to worry about money or the comforts of life. She would be treated like a queen, and I would still be able to see her. I would have access to the palace and to the power of Egypt. It could solve all our problems, and all it would cost is letting go of an impossible promise. It was not a bad way to live, but it was far from the best way to live. Good and not bad is often the enemy of the best. A kingdom on earth is the destination that threatens the kingdom of heaven. Lot thought that it was the thing to do. He congratulated me on the success of my strategy.

Have you ever been to Egypt?

Has earthly opportunity knocked on your door? Has a practical present been offered as the wise alternative to a "faith fantasy"?

Have you ever been to Egypt?

I should have been pleased with myself, but I was distraught, for I had placed the woman I loved in danger. To preserve my life, I had jeopardized my love. What kind of a man would do that? Have you ever taken things into your own hands and enabled a human-sized problem to become God-sized?

Pharaoh and Satan had manipulated the pieces on the game board of life, and God was in an unholy checkmate. If He let the scenario play out, Sarai would become Pharaoh's wife, and God's plan would be thwarted. If He effected Sarai's release, He would be rewarding a liar and circumventing consequences. How would that balance on the scales of justice?

I had let go of God's hand and taken things into my own, and it had become a disaster. I fell to my knees and reached up through the darkness. I could do nothing. I deserved nothing. I confessed everything and waited on the Lord.

I could never have anticipated His response. My hope was to escape with Sarai and the clothes on my back. Just survival. Just get me out of Egypt and let me start over again. I have learned my lesson.

God's plan was for abundance, not just survival. Plagues fell upon Pharaoh and all his household except Sarai. And when he found that she was a follower of God and my wife, Pharoah was furious. He probably would have killed me if it were not for the fear of more plagues. He gave me a good tongue-lashing and ordered his guards to deport our family.

He required us to leave. He wanted us to leave. He paid us to leave. He allowed us to keep everything. Sarah was able to take the gifts from the palace, and even Hagar her maid. I was allowed to keep the dowry.

It was amazing! I was overwhelmed by God's unexpected abundance. If I had been in His place and my chosen patriarch had strayed from me, I would have let the consequences play out and at least have taken away all his wealth. Let him face the potential of death. Shake him up so that he would remember never to stray again. Scare him good, but never reward him. Never make him rich. It would be the wrong message to send to a liar.

But that's why God is God, because He rises above the human tendency to administer justice and instead offers forgiveness. God's message to me was clear: "Don't try to work things out on your own. I have a plan. Rest in me, and I will provide." What amazing grace!

When we crossed the border of Egypt, I made a beeline for Bethel. I rebuilt the altar and worshiped. I came to God and found rest for my soul.

Have you ever been to Egypt?

The good news is that God can bring you back—back to the land of your first love, back to His house. Bethel means "the house of God." I was finally home. My restless heart found rest in Him.

Have you ever been to Bethel?

9

Egypt in My Home

IF SATAN CAN'T KEEP YOU IN EGYPT, he will seek to put Egypt into your home. It's one thing to let go of God and wander on Satan's soil, to live in Egypt. It's another to live in God's Promised Land but allow Egypt into your home.

Egypt and Canaan stand in stark contrast as two opposing philosophies of life. Forever incompatible, they stand beckoning humanity to follow different roads to happiness and fulfillment.

Egypt is the man-centered world where humans are worshiped. It is where you can make God in your image. The works of man are exalted, and humanism holds the answers to the questions of life. "We are our own salvation" is the mantra of this land. Every mystery of life can be explained starting with man. There is no room for a Creator, and the garden is a myth. Scientific theories are taken as fact to remove the hand of God from the origin of man.

Canaan is the Land of Promise, where God is the center of life and we are His children made in His image. Salvation is by "faith in Him alone." Humanity can add nothing—we are called to rely on Him. For faith to be complete, we need to embrace God's will according to His way and in His time. This is the land of promise, where men and women find their origin and meaning in the Creator.

The most subtle heresy is the mixture of the philosophies from both the land of man and the land of God. This is when faith is perverted by works and love is replaced by legalism. It is so engaging to think that we can help God.

It had been ten years since that first night that God spoke to me. This parchment had been retraced each year on the day that I set aside for the whole tribe to commemorate the promise. We called it the Festival of Hope, but each year our celebration seemed to lose a little of its energy.

Have you ever had to wait on the Lord?

The first year, everyone talked of the promise every day. Expectation, fervency, and hope glowed in our faces. The children of the servants asked me to tell the story every night around the campfire, and I often heard them reenacting it in their play. But as the years went by, doubt began to serrate the edges of our faith, and worship turned to ritual, confidence to questions, rest to restlessness. We still affirmed the promise, but our faith was attacked by time.

When we first received the promise, it took away that anxiety for Sarai and put her at rest. For nine years, she seemed to live in expectancy, but that seventy-fifth birthday reignited her worry. She began to talk about alternatives such as adoption or surrogates. I even talked to God about adopting Eliezer, the head of my household, as my heir.

The Lord reassured me that I would have a son. I wanted more than simply His word, so I asked for a sign. The Lord gave me the sign of a covenant.

We went through all the ceremonies of legal covenants. It was quite an experience. But Sarai had not experienced these encounters that strengthened my faith.

On the tenth year of the Festival of Hope, Sarai confirmed my fears. She told me that she was no longer able to have children. The impact on our faith was like the moment in a long distance race when you hit the wall. Your body seems unable to go on, and each stride is forced. We hit the wall of biology. We never expected that God would take this long to act. We were expecting a faith sprint, not a marathon.

Have you ever had to wait on the Lord?

Have you ever hit the wall of doubt? Have your problems ever seemed so great that your faith was eclipsed by the facts? Has the rest of faith turned to the restlessness of works?

It would only be a matter of time before the whispering gossips would pass the word about Sarai's condition. We would become the joke of the day. I can hear them now: "You know Abram and his wife Sarai. They live over in Bethel. I remember when they first moved here from Haran. I asked them why they had come to Canaan. Get this: Abram said it was because God had told him to move here. He claimed that God had talked to him late one night. I decided to play along with his story, so I asked him what God had said. And he told me God had promised to make him a great nation and give him descendants as the sand of the sea.

"I asked him if his wife was pregnant, and he said no, unfortunately she was barren. I asked him how old she was. He said 65, but he claimed that God had promised she would have a son. I could hardly keep a straight face. I advised him to keep the story to himself, but he and Sarai told it to everyone. In fact, they have a yearly festival to celebrate the promise.

"Well, guess what. Sarai's 75 now, and my wife just heard that she is no longer able to have children. They must feel like fools. Their God, Jehovah, has no power."

Have you ever had to wait on the Lord?

Has the passing of time caused you to question God?

Some people only added to our problems. Questions, suggestions, analysis, and jokes are the devil's tools to pry open the door of doubt.

Have you ever had to wait on the Lord?

Our faith was exhausted; our nerves were frayed. Sarai began to question whether I had heard God correctly. One of the women suggested to Sarai that God was waiting on us to do our part. After all,

God helps those who help themselves. Perhaps we were overlooking a very easy, simple solution that was obvious to people all around us—the Hagar solution.

It was the custom of Canaan for a woman who was barren to have children through her maid. This surrogate solution had never crossed my mind, but the more that Sarai talked about it, the more sense it made. It was a wonderful work-around. It would fulfill God's promise to us and save face among the pagans.

Have you ever tried to do God's will your way?

It never occurred to me that the Hagar solution was a mirror image of Sarai's Egyptian nightmare. If Satan can't get you to embrace humanism as your God, he will try to seduce you to mix it with your worship of God, turning faith to works and love to legalism. Satan has many roads to the exalting of the human and the diminishing of the divine. Through his cunning ways, he will either lead you to Egypt or lead Egypt to you.

Have you ever tired to do God's will your way?

I had no idea of the exhausting impact of doing God's will my way. From the first night I spent with Hagar, I knew things weren't right. The very thing God had rescued Sarai from in Egypt, we had willingly brought into our own home in Canaan. Egypt had adulterated the promise. The land of works had been transplanted to the land of promise and would deliver the child of works.

The moment it was apparent that Hagar was pregnant, her attitude toward Sarai changed. Instead of a maid simply giving birth to our child with Sarai as her mistress, Hagar assumed an attitude of superiority and disdain. The atmosphere around our camp was that of cold war. Tension, fueled by resentment and envy, filled the air.

Sarai suddenly lashed out at me with anger and bitterness. She blamed me for encouraging Hagar's attitude toward her. I'd never known Sarai to be bitter and envious. It shocked me. I told her that she was the mistress and that she could do as she pleased with Hagar.

Sarai treated her pretty roughly. It got so bad that Hagar ran away. Things have to get pretty bad for a pregnant woman to take the risk of traveling alone into the dessert. But that is exactly what Hagar choose to do. But the Lord intercepted her desperate journey at the spring near Shur. He spoke to her and told her to go back to Sarai and obey her—and then He told her to name her son Ishmael ("God hears").

It was an experience that Hagar prized. It demonstrates the extent of God's mercy. He reaches out to an Egyptian maid who is going to bear the child of works—a child that is neither of God's will or way. Yet He extends the promise into her life and gives her son a name of hope. No one is beyond the power of God to save. From this experience Hagar developed a special intimacy with God and a special name for Him. She called Him *Elroi,* which means "The God who sees."

Hagar returned to camp at God's command. A few weeks latter Ishmael was born, and it seemed as though our plan had worked out perfectly. I assumed that God was adding His blessing to my efforts, and I was once again satisfied with myself. Everyone seemed happy with the situation except Sarai, and I thought that it would just take her some time.

But suddenly God went silent.

Has God ever gone silent in your life?

From the time Ishmael was born, God didn't speak to me for almost thirteen years. Thirteen years! This was the spiritual desert of my life, and I didn't even realize it. I was so taken up with Ishmael.

I was so enamored with my fulfillment of God's promise that when God didn't speak to me, I thought it was because there was nothing more to tell me. I had no idea that He had another plan. I was satisfied—no, I was delighted—with Ishmael. I didn't realize that God could not accept my work as His. I thought I had done both of us a favor.

It was a wonderful work-around for an impossible problem, and I thought that Sarai and I had engineered it. But works—even good works—cannot achieve rest.

Rest is a result of faith, and works put the focus on us. They actually diminish faith in God as a source of life. His role as Saviour and Lord is subordinated to that of judge, simply declaring that our works are good. "Look God, no hands!" we say, as we ride triumphantly on the bicycle of life, having seemingly mastered the balancing act of living.

Behavior replaces belief; talent replaces trust. Religious teachers become spiritual taskmasters, enslaving their followers with the expectations of perfection to please a God of judgment. The spirit is exhausted, love is exchanged for labor, and God is silenced by the sad reality that His people settle for their good works as the highest goal of life. They try to live *for* Him, when He longs to live *in* them. They perform *good works* for Him, when He wants to perform *God works* in them.

Good works are so close to God works. They often look the same. They fit so well with the way people think about God. That is why they are so wrong. They distort divine love and form the basis of false religion. They are straight from Egypt, and they silence God.

For thirteen years, I was very satisfied with myself. Sarai was the only one who suffered. Egypt was in my home—and I welcomed it.

And God remained silent!

10

The Last Laugh

HAVE YOU EVER LAUGHED AT GOD?

I am not talking about laughing *with* God, but laughing *at* God.

Well, maybe not in His face—but have you laughed behind His back?

I was 99. It was the first time I had heard from God in thirteen years. A life of works had replaced faith, and I was at home with Ishmael. The excitement of a son had brought joy into my life. Sarai had accepted the solution as God's answer and judgment. Her hopes abandoned, she walked the death march of works. The very scheme she had devised to save face had resulted in losing faith. Numbed by human effort and only half fulfilled by human achievement, our faith turned into religion, and our visions of hope were exchanged for surrogate solutions.

Ishmael was our finest "work," but instead of being united through our efforts, our home was divided. And in "working" for God, we had lost Him.

I was making my nightly trip to the altar. I wasn't expecting to hear God's voice. Our last encounter was now only a distant memory. Ritual had replaced righteousness. Monologue had replaced dialogue. Life was so predictable; worship was so traditional. Night after night I walked the same path and mouthed the same words—and God remained silent.

Has your relationship with God ever become hard work?

Out of the night, as I mouthed my usual prayer of clichés, He spoke: "I am God Almighty. Walk before Me and be blameless, and I will establish my covenant between Me and you, and I will multiply you exceedingly." Genesis 17:1, 2.

I fell on my face. It was so refreshing to hear His voice again. It was almost like the days of old. I listened intently to every word as He spoke. It was the first time He referred to Himself as *El Shaddai*— God Almighty, able to do the impossible, with power over everything. I knew this was going to be a message of great importance.

He commanded me to walk before Him in total rest, 100 percent commitment, and total faith—nothing more. No works—just faith alone. And when He shared the rest of His commands, I understood why it would take total faith. They were so unbelievable that only faith or insanity would be able to embrace them.

Have you ever talked to yourself while listening to God?

My self-talk was an internal struggle to integrate the spiritual and the mental. When reason declares revelation unreal, self-talk becomes dissonant. I'll do my best to share what He said and how I felt.

"This is the time to fulfill My covenant with you," He stated, "and give you a son through Sarai."

"I don't think so," I thought. *"The time is past. Why have You put us through twenty-four years of waiting until Sarai is beyond giving birth? You know everything. You know what she told me at the festival. Don't try to raise my hopes again."*

My thoughts were interrupted as His instructions came: "Declare a family assembly. Change your name from Abram, ("Exalted Father") to Abraham, ("Father of a Multitude"). Change Sarai's name to Sarah, ("Princess—Mother of Nations").

The next few minutes with God were so incredible that I'd like to share our conversation:

Abraham: "OK, Lord, this is not going to be easy on me, but it will be humiliating for Sarah. I have really had to work hard to fulfill my current name, 'exalted father,' but when Ishmael was born, I could at least say I had one son. But this 'father of a multitude'—that's going to be a joke, and You'll be the laughing-stock of the gods.

"And Sarah—she is already the brunt of slurs and whispers. Everyone knows she is past childbearing age. Why not just leave her alone? She has finally accepted the fact that she will never have children. Don't make things worse by changing her name to 'mother of nations.' Why, that's almost a cruel joke!"

God: "I will bless Sarah, and kings of people will come from her."

Abraham: At that point, I was glad I was face down so God couldn't see me laugh at Him. This hurt so bad that it was either laugh or cry. What kind of sadist would tell an old barren woman who had accepted the fact that her dream of a child would only be fulfilled through her maid, that she was going to have a baby? How could I do this to Sarah?

I had watched time's cruel claws pry faith's fingers from the promise. I had seen hope turn to resignation and then die. I had watched it decay into cynicism. How could I dare try to resurrect its embalmed body with this impossible message?

It is not easy to carry a promise for twenty-four years. People loved to remind us that we told them God was going to give us a son. It's as if the oil in your lamp runs low, the flame flickers and dies, then someone comes along and calls you to believe again, and you refuse to be moved.

It's not that you don't want to believe, it's that you're afraid that it won't work out any better this time. The dream of a new life, of living in hope, has long been abandoned, and cynicism guards the door to your heart.

Has waiting on the Lord ever caused you to experience faith burnout?

Silent laughter shook my robe as I thought how this would play out in the real world. I could imagine assembling the family to tell them of God's commands. First I announce that God spoke to me last night. That would get their attention. I hadn't made that announcement in over thirteen years. Next, I would tell them that He said that Sarai would have a child—and that would bring snickering and a wave of wisecracks, followed by belly laughs.

But when I tell them that in honor of this coming event, God has given us new names—"Abraham, Father of a Multitude," and "Sarah, Princess—Mother of Nations—that would break up the meeting. Nobody could keep a straight face. Belly laughs for all.

When I finally composed myself and halted my laughter, I pled with God to accept Ishmael. I outlined the impossibility of a 100-year-old man and a 90-year-old barren woman, fifteen years post-menopause, having a son.

God: "No, Sarah will bear you a son, and you shall call his name Isaac."

Abraham: I didn't know how to react. God had rejected my reasoning and read my thoughts.

Sarah's son was to be called Isaac, which means, "he laughs." What I heard was, "I know how hard it's been for you to wait for My time. I know that over the years, your joyful laughter of hope has turned to sneers of cynicism because you don't want to cry. That's OK. You can share that with Me. I can handle the disappointment you have with Me, but be assured, the first laugh of joy that springs from your throat on the night of the promise will be fulfilled with the last laugh of rejoicing."

When I realized the meaning of "Isaac," I realized how much God had entered into my world—how fully He identified with my struggles. I rolled over, face up, and laughed with Him, face to face.

Have you ever laughed with God?

God: "As for Ishmael, I will bless him and make him a great nation, but my covenant will be with Isaac, and Sarah will bear a son in about one year."

Abraham: God was saying that Ishmael could never be the child of faith, because he was the child of my works. My best efforts, no matter how good, are never acceptable to God, who only accepts complete faith—all you know about yourself, committed to all you know about God. The desert of works had suddenly given way to the oasis of the Almighty. I was once again home with God.

Explaining to Sarai

Sarai tolerated my faith fantasy. She went through the motions of our renaming ceremony. She even allowed me to call her Sarah, but it was apparent she was guarding her emotions from another disappointment.

It all seemed so impossible.

Have you found it difficult to find your second wind of faith?

Somewhere in the journey of faith, you begin to work for God, and you exhaust your spirit. You accomplish good works, and they may have the outward appearance of God's works. But they are your Ishmael—your best effort to do God's will. And you awake one day to find that you have silenced God. You're still going through the motions of doing all the right things—the family altar, the festivals, the Sabbaths—but nothing is a delight. All is duty. You have hit the wall spiritually, and you're out of breath.

And then God speaks. He reignites the fire. You laugh and cry, and your heart burns within you. He breathes upon you, and you get His second wind. But you've got to choose to believe. And this time it may seem more impossible than the last, because time has erected greater barriers. Circumstances entreat you to settle for less. Just settle for a life of works. After all, it will all work out.

I could have refused God's second wind. I was comfortable with Ishmeal. He was a good boy, and I knew he would lead my family and perhaps create a nation. In the ways of earth, old men should not dream dreams, but the ways of heaven turn things upside down and include the word *impossible.* Isaac was to be my impossible faith child, and without my believing that, you would not be reading my story. I would have clung to the possible and missed the impossible.

Are you clinging to the possible?

Do you need a second wind of faith?

Listen to the whisper of El Shaddai—let the words fan the embers of faith smoldering beneath the ashes of your works. Laugh till it helps—live the impossible!

11

Snickers From the Kitchen

A FEW WEEKS LATER three travelers came down the road. It was a scorcher of a day, so I invited them to stop and rest—to eat and be refreshed. I didn't know at first that I was entertaining God, companioned by angels, but that was the case.

This visit of the Lord was to breathe hope into Sarah's heart. It was as if God were taking the extra time to revive a barren woman's faith—to allow her to see Him with her own eyes, to hear the promise and the prophecy with her own ears. This was Sarah's moment to laugh at God, to release her years of disappointment, and to laugh with God.

The meal was delicious. Sarah's spur-of-the-moment menu was a culinary delight. We ate outside under the oak at the entrance of our tent. A question became the turning point in our conversation. "Where is your wife, Sarah?" Two things struck me when God asked this question. First, it was obvious that He meant to get Sarah's attention—to signal His interest to her. And second, he called her by her promised name, Sarah.

"She is in the tent," I replied, noticing that Sarah had moved to the doorway in hopes of hearing more. The tent was right behind us. Sarah could easily hear the conversation.

"I will come back next year at this time, and Sarah, your wife, shall have a son."

There are some times when a veil is a real advantage, and this was one. It covered the repressed laughter that jiggled Sarah's robe. She turned and disguised it with a cough, to release the twenty-four years of disappointment. Her thoughts were no different than mine when I first heard God make the same promise.

The Lord read her thoughts and asked, "Why did Sarah laugh, saying 'I can't have children—I am too old?' Let me ask you—is anything too wonderful for the Lord?"

That closing phrase struck me, because the name God used for Himself was "the Creator God." It referred to His ability to speak things into existence, to form life from the dust of the ground. It signaled His power over nature. He had articulated Sarah's thoughts to let her know that He understood her disappointment and that it was all right to laugh at the promise. But this openness with God was so sudden, so accurate, so revealing, that it frightened Sarah.

It was God's intent to invite Sarah to be open with Him, to take away her anxiety and disappointment, to cast out her fear, so we could laugh together.

But Sarah responded, "I did not laugh." She was afraid to be open with God about her real feelings. I didn't know how God would respond to Sarah's denial. He could easily have shaken His finger in her face and accused her of lying. And He would have been absolutely accurate, but not necessarily loving.

His gentle reply addressed the issue and won her heart. "No, you did laugh, but that's OK." It took all the tension out of the air. God put her at ease. As He departed, He said, "Name him Isaac." As we walked away toward the road, I heard Sarah giggle and say quietly, "Isaac." Her delighted laugh reminded me of my youthful bride, full of life, full of hope.

When I returned to the tent, I knew things had changed for Sarah. The fragrance of spice filled the air. She appeared with mandrakes in her hand. Mandrakes are of special significance. They are the natural herb used to enhance fertility. Over the years, in our desperate attempts to have children, we tried almost every fertility aid known to man, from monitoring Sarah's temperature to ingesting herbs and potions. This imposed pressure had of course drained us of our spontaneous joy. Mechanics, formulas, advice and admonition, took the spontaneity from the physical love that had been so natural. I didn't want to return to that. I wanted to relax in the Lord, have confidence in His promise, and let Him bring it to pass. I looked at Sarah, lifted her veil, and whispered, "Isaac." I swept her into my arms and tossed the mandrakes into the corner. We fell on the bed in laughter.

12

The Promise Fulfilled

I LOVE THE WORD *IMPOSSIBLE*. It sets the stage for some of God's greatest acts, because it defines the situation as beyond human control.

Our finite limitations prepare us to receive the infinite. The impossibilities of earth are ready to be overcome by the possibilities of heaven. Against the backdrop of life's darkest impossibilities, when human solutions are impotent and human efforts are exhausted, there is only one place to go—to the Lord.

When God breaks through, all glory goes to Him. No human claim can be made for the victory.

The day we were sure that Sarah was pregnant was one of the most exciting of our lives. The possible had broken through the impossible. I called a family assembly, and with Sarah at my side, we made the announcement. There was rejoicing such as we had not seen since Hagar had become pregnant. But this was different. It was a praise service to our God—no human explanation, no Egyptian work-around. It was obvious that God had given life. Praise His name!

The word spread throughout the countryside, and our camp became a destination for kings and priests of every tribe around us. They would sit in wonder as I shared the story of our journey with Jehovah. I unfolded the drama, starting with the promise, and tracing our twenty-four years of waiting.

I shared how we had laughed at God's promise, and they couldn't believe that it was even thinkable to laugh at our God. They only appeased their gods, trembled at their altars, and expected punishment for their disobedience. Not one of them ever heard their god speak. I watched their faces fill with wonder as I described my relationship with Jehovah, but the part that truly overwhelmed them was when I told them the name God had given for our son. I loved that part!

They expected that God would punish me for laughing at Him, and I played on that expectation to demonstrate the differences between their gods and the God of love. "Do you know what God did when I laughed?" I asked the expectant listeners. They would respond with a flurry of guesses which revealed their fear of God. Not once did anyone come close to the truth.

Finally I would quiet them and break the suspense, "God told me to name our son 'he laughs.'" I threw back my head and laughed with all my joy.

The ending was so surprising—and so relieved their tension—that the tent exploded with laughter. At that point, Sarah would stand and verify the promise by her bulging profile.

Ninety and pregnant. Impossible!

13

The Birth of Isaac

HAVE YOUR EVER HAD A DAY IN YOUR LIFE so drenched with memories that you loved to replay it over and over in the theater of your mind?

I have. It was the day Isaac was born. I was so attuned to every detail of that joyous day that I can recall it in slow motion.

Have you ever waited for twenty-five years for a promise to come true? Expectations expand within your being until you can hardly contain them. Words such as *waiting* and *patience* betray the struggle between the desire to realize the promise and the understanding that it cannot be rushed. All promises come true in God's time. But when the day comes, it is so rich and wonderful that you will never forget it!

From the moment that Sarah began her labor, to the first cry of Isaac and the moment the midwife announced, "It's a boy!"—to the moment the carefully wrapped baby was placed into my arms—I will never forget that day.

During Sarah's labor I took down the parchment with the promise and retraced it on a larger sheet. This time I added a genealogy chart—Terah, Abraham, Isaac—and titled it "Forefathers of a Nation."

Only one thing clouded that day—the sense that Hagar and Ishmael were feeling disconnected, or worse yet, disenfranchised. I guess I really thought that we could all live together in harmony and that Isaac and Ishmael could grow up as brothers and friends.

I loved Ishmael. For twelve years he had been my answer to God's promise. He was the best thing that had happened to me in the first twenty-four years of living in Canaan, but I did not understand spiritual genetics.

As each act comes to life, it has a spiritual genetic code—faith or works. Ishmael was physically and spiritually linked to me. Physically, he was the child of my body, but spiritually, he was the child of my works. Isaac, on the other hand, was the child of God's working in my life. He was the child of faith.

I began to sense the mounting spiritual tension between the two mothers during Sarah's pregnancy. It was the same kind of tension that had plagued our home when Hagar was pregnant, but this time it was compounded by the fact that Ishmael was old enough to comprehend what was taking place.

Hagar was obviously coaching him, and he began to display attitudes of jealousy, envy, and covetousness. He was old enough to think about his birthright and inheritance, but Hagar seemed to make matters worse. She pressed me with questions about Ishmael's place in the family and about his inheritance. She constantly compared the two boys and pointed out all the ways in which Ishmael excelled.

Sarah began to pick up on Hagar's attitude, and she watched her like a hawk. I felt caught in an escalating emotional war. If looks could kill, our camp would have been the sight of a massacre. I couldn't do anything right. Giving attention to either boy offended the other mother.

This cold war was nerve-wracking. I could never be myself. Every action was twisted by an interpretation to prove that I was being unfair to someone.

Then Sarah dropped the bomb. It happened on the day of the feast to celebrate Isaac's passage from infant to toddler. It was our custom to celebrate the weaning of a child with a feast. I had done the same thing for Ishmael, but this feast seemed to bring out the worst in Ishmael. He was obviously fed up with the amount of attention Isaac was getting. I had to take him aside several times and talk to him about his behavior. I reminded him of how I had honored him with the same feast and that now it was Isaac's turn.

His sullen looks and cynical remarks told me he was hurting. I tried to hug him, but he ran away. I knew something was going to explode—I just didn't know when. It happened at the worst time, at the highlight of the ceremony, when Isaac was the center of attention.

Sarah had planned it carefully. We had practiced it privately. It was the moment that Isaac was to show how he was learning to walk, by taking his first steps from Sarah's arms to mine, and now Sarah and I got down on our knees a few feet apart. Sarah set Isaac up, and I held out my arms, saying, "Come to Daddy." Isaac's arms flailed with excitement. A grin spread over his face, and he took a few awkward steps toward my outstretched arms.

He swayed and started to fall, and I swept him up in my arms. His delighted laughter filled the air. The crowd was enchanted. They burst into applause and cheers, and Sarah's face glowed.

Suddenly Sarah's glow changed to anger. Her eyes fixed upon Ishmael, and everyone followed her gaze. There he was showing off in front of his friends by imitating Isaac's attempts to walk. He had a gift for impersonation, and everyone was entertained—everyone except Sarah. She was furious.

She had thought that when Isaac was born, public humiliation would be a thing of the past, but now it had ruined her party. Ishmael had made fun of her son. She had been the laughingstock of the community for too long, and she was unwilling for Isaac to be subjected to her experience.

She grabbed him from my arms and said, "You'd better deal with Ishmael. I won't have this in my home. He will not become our heir."

The party was over. The guests were stunned. Ishmael and his friends tried to keep a straight face, but their snickers betrayed their delight. Hagar stared daggers. I don't know what I said. I only remember how uncomfortable I felt as I dismissed the guests.

I told Ishmael I would deal with him later and went to find Sarah. I found her under the oak tree, holding Isaac. I approached, thinking that she had had time to settle down and regain her composure, but in reality, her momentary anger had hardened to resolve.

"Abraham, I want them out of our lives. We will never be able to build a home until they are gone. Ishmael can never be an equal heir with Isaac. Send them away."

I tried to reason with her, but she wouldn't listen. I had not seen Sarah this worked up since she drove Hagar away the first time. I was so disturbed that I turned and walked away. I needed time to think. Instinct led me down the path to the altar. I poured out my heart to God. "Lord, how can I get out of this dilemma? It's not fair to have to choose between my sons. I need them both."

"Abraham, Sarah is right. You need to send Hagar and Ishmael away. Ishmael is a child of your doing, your devising. A child of works. Isaac is the child of My doing, the child of faith. The spiritual roots of this nation must be faith. It can never be works. The road of faith is marked by altars of sacrifice, and today you must give up your best work, Ishmael, in order to build a nation of faith."

Stunned, I walked the path back to the camp, wondering how I would explain this to Ishmael and Hagar.

Have you ever had to say goodbye to someone you love?

It was more than goodbye—it was rejection, a parting that could never be reversed. My heart broke with the burden. I loved Ishmael. Twelve years of life shared as father and son can't be dismissed without great pain. No inheritance, no future in the chosen family—abandoned at 14. It all seemed so harsh. It tore my heart out to watch the servants pack.

I tried to explain to Ishmael that he would have his own nation, that God had promised it. But it didn't seem to matter. All he knew is that I was sending him away. He pleaded to stay, promising to treat

Isaac better and not cause any trouble. It was so hard to give him up—so hard to let go.

I sent them away. It was right, but it wasn't easy. By faith I sacrificed my greatest work. My arms embraced Ishmael. My eyes strained to watch his silhouette fade into the horizon.

Giving God your worst—your flaws, faults, and failures—is where faith's journey begins. Giving Him your best—your victories, your triumphs—opens you to the rest of the journey. To suffer the consequences of your mistakes is one thing. Turning your back on self-made victories is quite another.

Have you given up your "child of works"?

14

Home at Last

IT WAS JUST Sarah, Isaac, and me. I turned my attention to raising Isaac.

It had become a fun tradition for the children of the tribe to gather under our oak tree before bedtime, requesting to hear the story of the promise. I would hold Isaac on my lap and relate the incredible saga of how God spoke to me. Sarah would tell how she fixed dinner for God under this very tree.

Telling the story became a dramatic ritual, beginning with the inevitable request, "Tell us the story again, PLEASE!" and moving with a tempo of questions, interruptions, and prompts, always ending with laughter.

The questions:

"What did God look like?"

"Father Abraham, could you speak like God?"

"Would God ever talk to me?"

The interruptions:

"I think Pharaoh was a bad man for keeping Mother Sarah."

"I hope God asks me to fix dinner for Him."

The prompts:

"Mother Sarah, tell what it was like to be in Pharaoh's palace."

"Father Abraham, remember how you laughed at God?"

"Don't forget the part about changing your name. I love that part."

Isaac had a story like that of no other child.

When you tell a child that he or she is special, it builds self worth and confidence. As I watched Isaac grow, I remembered the day when he asked me if he could tell the story to the children.

I marveled at his poise as he unfolded every detail and fielded every question in the flickering light of the campfire. Sarah watched, wrapped in the pride of a mother listening to her only son.

And when he came to the end, he asked, "Do you know how to say my name?" And all the children chorused, "Isaac!"

To their surprise, he shook his head. "No, my name is not a word; it's a sound, and the way you get people to say it is with your fingers." He held up his hand and waved it in the air, then slowly advanced toward Sarah's feet.

The children squealed with anticipation, and Sarah began giggling. She is so ticklish, especially in her feet. Isaac grabbed her foot, and she began to laugh, and then a tickling match broke out around the campfire. Everyone laughed until they were exhausted.

Isaac was coming of age. From telling the story at the campfire, he progressed to other family leadership responsibilities.

He was my partner, my hope. I mentored him in faith, business, and culture. I provided opportunities for him to work in every phase of our family enterprise. My best leaders were his teachers as well.

I realized that I had been born when my father was much younger, and I had many more years to learn from him. I would not have the same luxury with Isaac. I made every minute count.

I took him with me to livestock auctions and counsels of kings. He was my constant companion. I loved that boy with all my heart. He was rapidly becoming a man, and I thoroughly enjoyed his development. It was as if all our dreams were coming true through Isaac.

A Voice in the Night

Have you ever awakened in the night with an eerie sense that something was outside? Have you ever felt compelled to go outside and investigate? Have you ever felt the strange calling of two forces as you ventured out—one, fight for your family, or two, run for your life?

I have. It was the middle of a dark night, and suddenly I awoke as wind shook the tent. I sat up and decided I had better go outside and see what was going on. As I stepped through the doorway, the clouds parted and the moon appeared, and thousands of stars sparkled against a black velvet sky.

Then I heard it—a voice whispering, "Abraham, Abraham." I realized it was my Lord. My fear changed to rapture as I awaited His words. I thought that God was going to give me instructions for Isaac's marriage. Sarah and I had been praying a lot about that lately. It was the one part of our dream as yet unfulfilled.

I answered, "Here I am," fully expecting God to reveal His marriage plans for Isaac. But His words were so different—so far from my expectations. They sounded more like a nightmare.

"Take now your son, your only son whom you love, Isaac, and go to the land of Moriah, and offer him there as a burnt offering on one of the mountains which I will tell you."

His words had surprised me in the past, but never like this. I was in shock. His presence faded, yet the words echoed, "Sacrifice your son."

I could think of a thousand arguments: "That's what the pagans do to appease their gods. You are not like that, Lord. You are love. I don't understand. This doesn't make sense. You give life—You don't take it away."

If I had not talked to Him and heard His voice so many times before, I would not have believed that this was God's voice. My heart raced with adrenaline as I repeated the words He had spoken. The command was clear but incomprehensible. The voice was familiar, but the request was foreign.

How could I sacrifice my own son? I could hardly bear the bloody experience with an animal, much less a person—much less Isaac. First I sacrificed Ishmael by sending him away. Now Isaac by putting him to death? Why would God ask such a thing?

I wandered in the darkness, pleading with God. When I was convinced that this was His will, I said no more. It was time to act, before Sarah was awake. She would never understand. The journey to Moriah would afford me time to talk to Isaac. I would make it simple now. We're going to worship God—a retreat of father and son to the mountain of the Lord. I awakened the servants first and informed them of my departure.

They hurriedly prepared the donkeys for the journey, and now it was time for Isaac. I hesitated as I stood beside his bed. The joy of my life—and I must wake him to begin this terrible task. "Son, wake up. You will need to get up. We need to go to the mountain of the Lord to worship together."

He responded willingly to my announcement. As he got ready, I took a sheet of parchment and quilled a message for my sleeping Sarah. When I finished, I hung it just beneath the promise. I knew she read it everyday and would find the message.

Taking Isaac on a pilgrimage to worship God in the mountains. We will return by the end of the week. Pray that this will be all that God intended for Isaac. Shalom.

As he finished loading the donkeys, one servant motioned me aside. "Sir, you split the wood, you filled the fire urn, but where is the lamb?"

Instinctively I whispered, "God will provide." He didn't understand, but he did accept.

I overheard him whisper to his coworker. "He said, 'God will provide.'"

We traveled a good distance before dawn, and as the sun arose, we crested a hill and looked back to see our encampment glistening in the sunrise. If Sarah only knew about my mission this day! How would I ever explain taking her only son's life?

I could hardly say a word as I contemplated the thought. We rode on in silence. It was the longest two days of my life. Every night I got up after the others went to sleep, and I pled with God for another plan. I had refused to take a lamb, to remove the possibility of losing courage and offering it instead of Isaac.

Fear begat doubt and a myriad of questions. " Isn't there another way, Lord? How can you create a nation without Isaac?"

Questions and arguments were replaced by pleadings. "Please, Lord, let him live." And finally bargaining. "Could Isaac sacrifice me? I am old, and my life has been given to preparing him to lead a nation. Sacrifice me, Lord."

It was an exhausting test. Mountains in the daylight—intercession in the darkness. I wore out my body in the light and my spirit in the night. I put blisters on my feet walking and calluses on my knees praying.

The second night, the breakthrough came. Without an audible word from God, my anxieties subsided, fear fled, and a peace came over me that I cannot explain. I felt God fill me with His Sabbath rest. His spirit embraced mine, and I knew everything would be all right.

It suddenly occurred to me that God had the power to bring Isaac back to life. The more I entertained that thought, the more I became convicted that this was His plan. A miracle for Isaac, so that he would have no fear. He would know God's power. He would have an indelible understanding of omnipotence. My spirit shouted, "Jehovah Jireh—God will provide." You can face any trial, any tragedy, any temptation, knowing that God will provide. You can endure life's journey if you know the destination is victory.

For the first time in three nights, I could relax. Faith begat rest, rest begat peace, peace begat sleep. Heaven's alarm stirred me from my sleep. God had promised to show me the place where I was to sacrifice Isaac.

As the sun rose, its first rays seemed to focus like a laser pointer on one part of the mountains. The question of location was clear—the last evidence of His leading complete. Now my attention turned to how I was going to tell Isaac.

Today, there would be no laughter in his name. We must be alone—father and son. I asked the servants to stay at the base camp while we went on to worship. "We will return." Not just me, but both of us.

As we began the climb, Isaac was the first to speak. His question set the stage for our most memorable talk. "Father, I see the wood and the fire, but where is the lamb?" Full of calm and confidence, I responded, "Jehovah Jireh—God will provide."

And then I began to remind him of all the ways our family had been led by relying on that one belief—that God would provide. Confidence grows in the sunlight of faith's memories. As we recalled God's leading in our lives, I emphasized the importance of the altar.

As we talked, I realized that this was the day that Isaac would receive his spiritual birthright. The day of his first altar and my last. Today, the torch of faith would be held by the hand of both father and son. This day it would burn bright from generation to generation.

Faith would make our nation eternal, yet it must not be forced. It must be freely chosen. I returned to address his question, "Where is the lamb?" My answer—Jehovah Jireh—must be explained. The horror of the knife must be comprehended, the gruesomeness of death absorbed, trust in God's commands confirmed. The confidence that we would return together, if necessary by resurrection, must be shared. The recognition that nothing is too hard for the Lord must wrap every question, absorb every doubt, and exalt our faith.

In a half-day climb, Isaac had to deal with all the questions, emotions, and temptations that had taken me two days to resolve. From our brief conversation together, Isaac had to accept that I had heard God correctly.

My salvation was in repeating my belief—God will provide. It was God's tranquilizer for this trauma. The closer we got to the summit, the more the horror of human sacrifice gripped my imagination.

How could I bear the first act of the knife, with its bloody consequence? How could I light the fire, when I could hardly bear the smell of animal hides burning? But the smell of pagans' human sacrifices engulfed my olfactory memory. I was overcome by nausea, and we stopped for a breather. With my head in my hands, I was ready to shout, "It's too much, Lord!" when faith whispered, "God will provide." Isaac interrupted my thoughts, "Dad, it's all right. We can do this together. God has a reason. We may not see it right now, but we will in time."

"Thank you, son. Give me a hand. We'll be on our way."

"Father, you know I'm scared. I don't want to die. It's the knife that scares me most. I don't want to have you cut my throat. It takes too long to die. Is there a quicker way?"

"Yes, my son, a blow to the heart would make it quicker."

"Could we do it that way?"

"Of course, Isaac."

"Father, I want this to be our altar. I want to bring you the rocks, and you put them in place."

"Isaac, I want you to know that I asked God to let me be the burnt offering. I can't imagine hurting you. Since your were born, I have been your protector. How can I do this to you?"

"You're not doing it to me. We're doing it together, because we believe in doing what God says. But Father, you need to answer me one more question."

"Yes, of course, what is it?"

"When you left the servants this morning, you told them we would go and worship and that we would return. Yet you knew what God had commanded, so why didn't you say, 'I will return?' Were you just keeping them from getting suspicious?"

"No, my son, I meant what I said. You see, late last night as I agonized with God, I suddenly felt God's rest. Nothing had changed. He had not revoked His command, but I felt closer to God than I ever had before. I realized that God, who had brought you into this world through a miracle, could bring you back to life. I knew in that instant that He might have another miracle in store for us—resurrection."

"What do you mean, resurrection?"

"It means coming back to life."

"Has it ever happened before?"

"No, not that I know of."

"Then how could you believe that it would happen now?"

"Because I have the same peace I felt when God told me I would have a son. I just believe that God will provide. It suddenly clicked. That's why He had us go to the land of Moriah. The name is like a seed of hope in a command of despair. It is the only thing that I have had to cling to for the last two days. Moriah. It means, 'it will be provided in the mountain of the Lord.'"

"You want me to believe in something I have never seen, resurrection, because you heard God say one word, *Moriah?*"

"Isaac, I know it's difficult, and even beyond belief, but every good thing in our lives is beyond belief—our home, our family, and you. But you need time to think, to talk with God. This must not be just my belief. It must be yours as well."

"Pray for me, my father. Pray right now before we reach the place."

"Oh, Jehovah-Jireh, I stand here with my son in my arms—the son You provided according to Your promise. And because of Your command, we have climbed this mountain to worship You, to offer up to You my only son. O Lord, if it is possible that this is not your will, speak now, Lord."

"Father, I hear only the wind. Is God's voice in the wind?"

"No, my son, God's voice is not in the wind."

"Then it is His will, Father—it is His will. We must go on. Can you help me get the wood back in place? God will provide. Let's climb the mountain, Father."

15

God's View of Moriah

I HAVE BEEN WATCHING Abraham and Isaac for the past two days, but this third day has torn at My heart.

As they grow in faith, you watch your children climb life's most difficult mountains. And as Abraham prayed, I drew closer. This father and son were climbing beyond reason, beyond emotion, to the summit of faith, where full dependence meets full assurance and holy fire ignites the human heart with love's eternal flame.

You may wonder why I didn't stop them. Why did I let them go to the brink of death?

Simply to allow them to experience full faith. Their acts of faith are the essence of worship. Therefore, I would make this the national center for worship—the place where the temple would be built. Moriah is the place of worship. The point of sacred sacrifice is the intersection where God gives all to man and man gives all to God.

Abraham and Isaac climbing the mountain of sacrifice was but a foretaste of the experience I would have years later on a nearby mountain as My Son climbed alone. The dynamics were so similar. Isaac's back was loaded with a bundle of wood. Jesus' back supported a cross of wood.

I held My breath as I watched this drama of Abraham and Isaac unfold. Their prayer drew Me so close, its pathos but a forecast of the words that would come from My own Son's lips. Together in the night, We would struggle, He in My arms, as salvation's hope called for sacrifice without reprieve.

I wanted to shout to Abraham, "It's enough. You have gone far enough!" But I knew that faith could not be final until he put everything on the altar, nothing held back. That would be true worship. That would be Sabbath rest.

I hovered close to Moriah's summit as father and son arrived. "Isaac, this is the place, my son. We will build the altar here. Let's gather the stones."

Silently the altar is erected, and the father turns to the son. "I brought a cloth to cover your eyes and some cord to bind your arms. It will make it easier on both of us."

"Use the cord, Father. Bind me tight, but don't use the cloth. I want to see your face until the last. I want to hear you say again that God will provide."

"You must help me, my son. You must say it with me. If I did not believe that God will provide, I could never do this to you."

"Let's shout it together, Father. As you plunge the knife, tell me once more of your belief about the resurrection."

"Oh, my son, you are a gift from God, and I am convinced that if He brought you to life once, He will do it again."

"But, Father, if God is going to resurrect me, why sacrifice me? Just let me live."

"No, Isaac, the sacrifice is a demonstration of our belief in God's ability to handle death. It is our worship."

"Bind me, then, Father. God will provide. Bind my hands and my feet. Tighter, tighter. It feels too loose. There, that's fine. Now help me onto the altar."

"All right, I am ready. Go ahead, Father."

I watch the old man reach for the knife, grip it in his hand by his side, and turn his face toward the heavens and pray, "O Lord, we have done as You have commanded. I have brought my son, my only son, to Your mountain to sacrifice, because I have come to believe that You are a God of life and love. Isaac and I freely give ourselves to You this day. I raise the knife of death, because I believe You will provide."

"Abraham, Abraham! Stop! Don't strike him! Your faith is full. You have held back nothing. Look over in the bush—I have provided a ram."

"I don't see anything. Isaac, do you see a ram?"

"Yes, Father, I see it, I see it! Jehovah-Jireh—I AM ALIVE! I AM ALIVE! Praise God! Cut me loose, Father. I will get the ram."

I join the angel choir in a song of praise as all heaven is transfixed on Abraham and Isaac's long embrace. The celebration of life subsides, and the ram is prepared for sacrifice. Father and son kneel beside the altar in thanksgiving.

"O Jehovah Jireh, how great is Your name. You have spared my son Isaac. Thank you, Lord! Yes, God of my Father, You have brought us here to worship, and I have experienced the power of faith. I have returned my only son Isaac into Your hands, and You have shown Your love. You have tested our faith, and we have tested Your love. We have *rested* in You, and You have provided for us.

Resting in the Creator-God is the foundation of worship. Sabbath rest is the summit of faith! When faith is full, rest is complete, and Sabbath is eternal. It can transform your life. Walk it daily, celebrate it weekly. Give everything to God—receive everything from God. And REST!

POSTSCRIPT: *Moriah became the sacred ground for Solomon's Temple, sanctified by the faith of Abraham and Isaac. It would be the place of Sabbath Rest for all Israel.*

Experiencing
Sabbath Rest

SABBATH REST . . . to stop, relax, and draw close to Jesus—to drink in the victory and live with God-confidence.

Examples of ways to experience Sabbath rest:

1. We create an ambience for welcoming the Sabbath at sunset on Friday, using all the five senses:

   • Beautiful spiritual music filling the house.

   • Having a special place to watch the sun setting as we anticipate a beautiful 24 hours.

   • The lighting of special scented Sabbath candles throughout the house—we have a menorah and many other candles. (Candles represent warmth, closeness, and peace.)

   • Fresh flowers.

   • "Tradition meal"—ours is, and has been for more than fifteen years, tortillas and all the fixings.

   • Special drink—sparkling grape juice (about ten years ago, our daughter suggested grape juice, because of its symbolism of freedom, joy, and forgiveness.)

• Sabbath placemats and napkins complete the setting.

2. Before our meal, we repeat the Sabbath commandment, complete with hand motions. This has become a fun tradition in our family.

3. One of our favorite questions to ask each other at our Friday evening meal is: "How did you see Jesus this week?"

4. A favorite tradition began when the children were younger and has carried forth even as they were away in college. That is to give them "Sabbath Surprises." First, we start with a decorated "tin bucket" in which we placed these surprises. Here are some examples of our surprises over the years, according to the children's ages and likes: scented soaps, sticker books/stickers, pipe cleaners, colored pencils, barrettes, hair combs, gum, mints, bubble bath, yogurt, raisins, books, picture frames, collectible items, perfumes, colognes, film, CDs, socks, ties, belts, stamps, personalized note paper, a sketch pad, and so on. On holiday Sabbaths, we gave items that could be used to create a gift for another person. Our goal was to create positive anticipation of the Sabbath and also to give something that was practical, age-appropriate, and that could be used Friday evening, at church, or for a Sabbath afternoon activity.

5. After our Friday night meal, when the kids were small, we'd all pile into our bed, and with the lights out and the candles burning, we'd talk about the week and ask forgiveness of each other if needed. Many times we'd listen to Bible stories on the Christian radio or via tape.

How to extend "Sabbath Rest" beyond the twenty-four hours of the Sabbath to the rest of the week:

1. We establish visual, daily reminders of God's promises: We write Bible promises on Post-It notes and put them all over the house—such as on the refrigerator, bulletin board, bathroom mirrors, and the children's closets. They also work nicely on the car dashboard or rearview mirror, in your mate's briefcase, and in the children's lunch box or schoolbooks. We've shared many stories as

a family of how God has used these texts at just the times we needed them, and it reminded us of "Sabbath Rest."

2. We create "Answered Prayer" photo albums. Many years ago, we realized that we took lots of photos of various milestones and accomplishments in our lives, so why not take pictures of our spiritual milestones in answered prayer? Here are a few of the photos we have in our album:

• Our son and a coral snake in a stump.

• Our daughter and her dad with a golf club.

• Our son and a friend with a flashlight shining in the dirt at Yellowstone National Park.

• One parent with a lost but found $20 bill.

• An empty typewriter case with a blue angel airplane.

• One parent with a scorpion on a chair.

• Our daughter and her long-lost Bible.

There are many other pictures—each with a story. These visual reminders of God's presence not only encourage us as individual family members but present beautiful opportunities to share with friends and other family members.

3. Other ways that our friends have used to record their spiritual milestones or answers to prayer include:

• Photos/writing on their waterski.

• Carving dates onto a cane or rustic mantle.

• Painting them onto rocks.

The Journey to Blessing

16

The Sabbath Is Heaven's Hug

IN SCRIPTURE, GOD USES the word *blessing* to indicate His love for us.

Karl Barth, the renowned German theologian, was asked to sum up the gospel in one sentence. His response: "Jesus loves me, this I know." The realization that God loves us just as we are is a ringing endorsement of our worth. The Sabbath blessing is designed to instill this sense of eternal worth into your life and mine. God instructed the priests to pronounce the following Sabbath blessing upon the people:

"The Lord bless you, and watch over you; the Lord make His face shine upon you and be gracious to you; the Lord look kindly on you and give you peace." Numbers 6:24-26.

This text portrays God as a proud Father smiling down upon His children. It is through the eyes and facial expressions that we read the heart of a person. And the Sabbath blessing reveals God's admiring gaze and smiling face.

Too many people envision God's scowl, and too few enjoy His

smile. Martin Luther was one of those people. His earthly father wanted him to become a lawyer, and when Martin chose instead to be a priest, his father disapproved. Over the years, his father criticized and shamed Martin. It affected Martin's view of God to the extent that he said it was difficult for him to pray the Lord's Prayer, because it began with the words, "Our Father, who art in heaven." Never knowing the acceptance of an earthly father caused him to doubt the heavenly father's acceptance.

In a worth-draining world, God stands ready to give you heaven's hug—and punctuates that fact by His Sabbath blessing. He planned it into the day, and He looks forward to reaffirming your worth. Sabbath is our personal "Mount of Transfiguration"—the place where we hear our heavenly Father say, "This is My beloved child." If you have not experienced the acceptance of an earthly father, then the Sabbath blessing is doubly important for you. For your Heavenly Father will provide the blessing that your earthly father never gave you and will heal your wounded worth.

God intended that each child should be blessed by his or her earthly father. But sin attacked His intention, and today too many fathers abandon or abuse their children, thus wounding not only their body but their spirit. Too many fathers criticize one child and praise another. Too many fathers have wounded worth from their own past that has never been healed by the Sabbath blessing, and they are therefore unable to bless their kids. If you come from one of these settings, whether you are a father or a child, this section is especially for you. The lives of Jacob and Leah unfold the tragedy of how earthly fathers can hurt their children—and reveal the triumph of how the heavenly Father can restore the blessing.

In "Experiencing Sabbath Blessing" following chapter 19, you will learn how to bless your family. One of the most meaningful ways to begin the Sabbath each week is for the parents to bless their children. It was Hebrew tradition that at the beginning of Sabbath the father of the house blessed each of his children. I envision him starting with the youngest child, and gathering each child in turn into his arms, looking into their eyes, and sharing his love and hope for them. Gary Smalley has outlined this process in his book, *The Blessing*. I have adopted it for my family. When you start the Sabbath by blessing your family and your spouse, it sets a tone of personal affirmation that bonds you to them. I believe that this tradition can create a spiritual unity that will be recalled with each setting of the sun on Friday evening. It will form an eternal reminder of your priceless value. Yes, Jesus loves me, this I know!

The hug of your heavenly Father is awaiting you in the Sabbath Blessing.

17

A Bad Beginning

JACOB'S STORY BEGINS in Genesis 25:21: "And Isaac prayed to the Lord on behalf of his wife because she was barren, and the Lord answered him, and Rebekah, his wife, conceived. And she said, 'If it is so, Lord, why then am I this way?' So she went to inquire of the Lord, and the Lord said to her, 'Two nations are in your womb. Two peoples shall be separated from your body, and the one people shall be stronger than the other, and the older shall serve the younger.'

"When her days to be delivered were fulfilled, behold, there were twins in her womb, and the first came out all red like a hairy garment, and they named him Esau, and afterward his brother came forth, and his hand was holding onto Esau's heel, so his name was called Jacob."

Have you ever wondered how some parents come up with the names they give their children? This is one of those situations. God told them they were going to have twin sons. Even with this heavenly sonogram, they somehow didn't use the information to do such a basic task as selecting names for the boys. It is hard to believe that

Isaac and Rebekah left the naming of their children until the moment of birth, but that appears to be what happened.

First comes Esau. He is red—he is hairy. So they call him "red hairy," which is the meaning of Esau.

Second, as Esau is being born, the hand of his twin brother reaches out and grabs his heel. Instantly, Jacob names him "heel grabber." For short, they simply call him "heel."

What a terrible name! How would being called a "heel" affect you every day of your life? This name would plague Jacob's life. It has carried its impact even into our day, as people came to refer to a person who cannot be trusted as a "heel." It's a name that would be used as a curse by Jacob's brother and the entire community.

It's bad enough to be called a heel, but the real tragedy of this story is found in how Isaac related to the two boys. "When they became youth, Esau was a skillful hunter, a man of the field; but Jacob was a peaceful man living in tents. Now, Isaac loved Esau because he had a taste for the game, but Rebekah loved Jacob."

Picture it—you are growing up, and you're a "chip off the old block." You are Dad's favorite son. These were the terms people used to describe Esau. When it was time to go hunting, Isaac chose to take Esau and leave Jacob. Jacob not only had a bad name, he had a different temperament. He was not macho—not the aggressive hunter. He was more quiet, so he was adopted by his mother, and scripture records that Rebekah loved Jacob, while Isaac loved Esau.

Earthly fathers make a tragic mistake when they show favoritism to their children, for one feels fully blessed while the other feels shame and worthlessness. I can imagine what it was like when they got ready to go on a hunt, and Esau was the one taken while Jacob was left behind.

Every boy longs to be his father's favorite. For Jacob, it will never be. Therefore his need for blessing goes unfulfilled, his worth shrinks, and he consoles himself with dreams of his fathers blessing. But reality shatters dreams, and hope is replaced by hurt.

Rebekah consoles him with the prophecy that he will be the stronger of the two brothers. She continually reminds him that He is God's favorite. The days and years pass by, and nothing changes. The bond between Isaac and Esau grows stronger, and Jacob's self-worth steadily diminishes.

One day, Rebekah overhears Isaac speaking to Esau, saying, "Go—I'm getting old, and my eyesight is almost gone. I can barely see. I have no idea when I'm going to die, but I'm going to enjoy giving you my blessing right now while I still have the strength. Go hunting for me and get a deer. You know how I love venison. You're a great hunter, Esau. Cook it, and we'll have a feast, and I will bless you."

As Rebekah hears these words and watches Esau depart, she realizes the time is critical. She calls Jacob and says, "This is your moment. This is when you can receive the blessing." She spins a scheme of how Jacob can supplant Esau and receive the blessing. They execute it flawlessly. It works, and Jacob now kneels before his father, pretending to be Esau. Dressed in his clothes, disguised by goatskins, he feels the longed-for blessing as his father places his hands upon his head and prays a prayer of prophecy about his future.

It is the moment he has dreamed for. It should be the happiest moment of his life, but as he leaves the tent, he feels empty. For the truth is, the only time that Jacob knew what it was like to feel his father's blessing was when he dressed up like his brother. For the first time, he feels all the impact of his name ("heel"). His worth is drained from his being. For in the final quest for his father's favor, he has sacrificed his self respect. And self-respect is the raw material of self-worth.

It didn't take long before Esau returned and discovered the plot. His cries rang from the tent, "Bless me—oh, my father, bless me!" Yet the blessing had been given to Jacob, so Esau vowed he would kill his brother after his father's death.

Rebekah admonished Jacob to run for his life, and in the stillness of the night she quietly weeps as she packs his belongings. Isaac is told that his son Jacob is leaving, and for the first time he gives him a token blessing. To Jacob it must seem like the hollow obligation of a father who would prefer to bestow it upon his favorite son. This symbol of love without substance cuts deeper into Jacob's wounded worth. It is like celebrating an anniversary when the marriage has gone stale.

He embraces his mother for the last time and slips out of town. Jacob's heart pounds with the fear that Esau might discover that he is alone. He runs across the rough terrain, traveling deep into the night until he is exhausted, and comes to a plateau on the plain of Luz. The depth of his depression is apparent by his actions. The darkest night any of us face is when we have betrayed ourselves and lost our self-respect. Exhausted physically by travel, exhausted spiritually by shame, Jacob collapses on a pile of rocks and chooses a rock for a pillow.

It is obvious he is not a hunter. Any good hunter knows how to choose a bed in the wild. It's obvious that he is depressed. Why would anyone choose a rock for a pillow?

His actions betray the fact that he was ashamed of himself. That night, he was homeless. The one person he knew loved him had kissed him goodbye. The one whom he had hoped would bless him, he had deceived. He has been without a father, but this night will be his first without a mother. His prayers are groans and moans pleading for forgiveness. The tears course down his cheeks and drop on the cold stone to the dessert floor.

It is the midnight of his life—the midnight of shame. But Jacob doesn't know that he has a heavenly Father who loves him and is about to break the cycle of shame with the power of blessing. Jacob has fulfilled his name, and he feels like a heel. Shame replays the chronicle of his crime, and guilt casts its shadow of despair across his soul as the darkness of discouragement engulfs his spirit. It is the devil's night, but not for long. Jacob's nightmare of shame is about to be replaced by the heavenly Father's blessing.

And Jacob had a dream (Genesis 28:12): "And behold, a ladder was set on the earth with its top reaching to heaven, and, behold the angels of God were ascending and descending on it. And, behold, the Lord stood above it, and said, 'I am the Lord the God of your father Abraham and the God of Isaac. The land on which you lie, I will give it to you and to your descendants, and your descendants will also be like the dust of the earth, and you shall spread out to the west, and to the east, and to the north, and to the south: and in you and in your descendants shall all the families of the earth be blessed. Behold, I am with you, and will keep you wherever you go and will bring you back into this land, and I will not leave you until I have done what I have promised you.' And Jacob awoke from his sleep and said, 'Surely the Lord is in this place, and I did not know it.'

"And he was filled with awe, and he said, 'How awesome is this place, and this is none other than the house of God, and this is the gate of heaven.'"

God's blessing changes everything, because it takes away the shame and fills you up with worth. And when that happens, your circumstances are transformed. Just a few hours earlier, Jacob had been a fatherless son sleeping in an open field, overwhelmed by shame. The Father's blessing transformed everything: Jacob's identity changed from unloved outcast to patriarch standing in the lineage of Abraham and Isaac as God's chosen leader. The plain of Luz changed to the promised land. The rock pile changed to the house of God. Sin's hideout changed to heaven's gates.

Had the circumstances changed?

No, only his view had changed, for when you realize you are loved by a heavenly Father, you can rise above your earthly situation, for you are a child of the King, and you rename your circumstances. Jacob arose and renamed the place Bethel, for he said, "This is the house of God."

From homeless to the house of God. From the gates of hell to heaven. This is the power of the blessing, and out of that sense of God's love for him, Jacob promised to return to God a gift of tithe, for when God fills you up with spiritual worth, you want to return to Him some of your earthly worth as a symbol of His blessing in your life. Jacob arises and begins a new life—a life under the blessing of a heavenly father. A life that will be absent from an earthly father but filled with the presence of a heavenly Father. Estranged on earth—affirmed of heaven.

He has found his eternal home, and his spirit is renewed. He has a heavenly Father, but the challenges are far from finished. The difficulties are far from removed, because the lack of an earthly father's blessing leaves many scars and much pain to be worked through. For Jacob it would be a process, a pilgrimage, a challenge that would go on throughout his life. Two opposing forces would pull on his spirit—sin's shame seeking to drag him down, and the Father's blessing seeking to lift him up. The same is true for all of us, and this is why God created Sabbath.

The Sabbath is designed to give us a time to settle down with a loving Father and hear His affirmation. We need the Sabbath blessing the most when we have failed to live with worth or when we have been devalued by our own acts. This is when the world will shout shame into our ears; this is when Satan will whisper shame into our spirits. And this is when God draws near with heaven's dream of blessing. But unless we shut out the voices of shame and listen for the Father's blessing, we will never hear it.

Quiet now—no other voices. "Listen up," and hear His voice. "Look up," and see the Father's smile. This is the end of a nightmare and the beginning of a dream. This is your Sabbath blessing!

18

A Woman Shamed

JACOB'S JOURNEY FROM LUZ took him to his uncle's home. There by a well, he met Rachel, the favorite daughter of Laban. It was love at first sight.

The scripture says she was "beautiful of face and form," and Laban knew her value, for the value of a beautiful daughter was expressed in the dowry she could obtain as a wife. She could no doubt receive the hand of a prince and the dowry of a princess.

Jacob had no right to ask for her hand, since he had no financial worth. But when you have the dream of being the father of a great nation, when you know that God has promised you a land, it changes your self-perception. Thus he boldly approached Laban to ask for her hand.

Laban struck a bargain with this confident young man. Seven years of labor for Rachel's hand. So Jacob set out to fulfill the seven years, and the Bible says that those seven years seemed but a few days because of his love for Rachel.

When he finally marked off the last day on his calendar, he went to Laban and said, "My time is complete. I want the wedding." So the preparations began.

Rachel's anticipation and excitement and joy for her marriage ceremony stand in stark contrast to her older sister Leah. You see, the saga of this household was the sage of two sisters: Leah, like Jacob, was unloved. Rachel, like Esau, was loved by her father.

Unfortunately, at this period in history, the evaluation of a woman was based on her beauty, and Leah's weak eyes stood in contrast to Rachel's beauty. Throughout her life, she played the role of the plain sister. Just once, she would like to have heard some man talking favorably about her. Just once, she would like to have been able to cry in her father's arms about how boys were mean and have him wipe her tears and bless her with affirmation. Just once. But it never happened.

In fact, quite the contrary. Over the years, Laban made it plain that she was not marketable as a potential wife. Then he trapped her in the double bind of public shame as he told her what a public disgrace it would be for her younger sister to be first to the altar. From the day that Jacob asked to marry Rachel, Laban intensified his attack on Leah's worth. "When are you going to get married, Leah? I certainly hope it is before Rachel. It would be a disgrace for your younger sister to get married before you do."

This nagging question became the primary point of discussion with her father, and the pain caused Leah to avoid him when possible. Because he also prompted other family members to approach her, she could not escape this countdown to Rachel's joy and her own shame. Rachel had always been the favorite, and Leah had learned to cope with this fact of life. Her friends and other family members had become a shelter for her worth. But now everywhere she turns, the "question" is the agenda. There is no escape! Now the inevitable had arrived—how could she endure it?

The traditionally prepared wedding feast went on for seven days. About halfway through the feast, the wedding took place. The night of the wedding, the bride would be taken into the groom's tent, and then he would join her for the consummation of the marriage. Leah knew that her role as sister of the bride would add only pain. Since they had been little girls, she and Rachel had practiced playing one of their favorite games—the wedding. And the highlight of the game was always getting ready for the groom. Their pretend game had been filled with giggles and laughter as they helped each other get dressed and imagined which of the village's boys would be entering the tent to sweep them into his arms to live happily ever after.

But now reality crushed all the fun out of their pretend world as Leah sits dutifully waiting for Rachel. She is prepared to help her get dressed, but she is unprepared for the final attack on her worth. She steels her spirit for one more assault from her father as he enters the tent with Rachel on her arm. They are all laughter and smiles, and she is thankful that her veil covers her silent tears and red eyes of disappointment. It has all happened just as her father predicted. No one wants to marry Leah.

That night, all the forces of evil, all the shame of Satan, were heaped upon Leah through the words of her father. We do not know what was said as Rachel and Leah stood in their father's tent, for Rachel would be dressed with the bride's garments, perfumed with exquisite scents, and led privately to the bridegroom's tent. While the wedding party carried on their feasting through the evening, the bride was being prepared for her wedding night.

In the midst of the preparation, an encounter took place between three people—Laban, Rachel, and Leah. This was a sad encounter involving the destruction of a woman's value. It must have gone something like this:

"Leah, you know I have tried every way I know to find a husband who is willing to pay a dowry for you, and it just has not come to pass. Rachel, tonight is your wedding night, but it will be a shame if you are married before your sister. It will be a disgrace on our family. It is not heard of in our community. It is not acceptable."

"What would you want me to do, Father?"

"Just this once, for your sister Leah, let her wear the wedding gown. Let her go into the wedding tent. Let her take your place."

"Father, it is my wedding night. I love Jacob. We've waited for this night for seven years—how can you ask me to do this?"

"Yes, Rachel, but think of poor Leah."

"Father, Rachel doesn't have to think of me or feel sorry for me, and I do not want to have this conversation."

"Leah, listen to me. I am your father. You will do as I say. If you want ever to have a man, this is the night, and this is the way."

So through a sad dialogue, a woman is convinced that she will never be able to experience love unless she deceives a man by dressing up to be her sister. The final attack on her worth is orchestrated by her father as he appeals to Rachel's sense of pity for Leah. Pity is the final proof of worthlessness, and Leah's spirit is limp.

This is the night when the devil will rejoice, for what goes around comes around. He will get two birds with one stone. He will forever remind Jacob of his deception by paying back with deception. And he will forever lock Leah into a life of shame by giving her a marriage without love. I believe that the way Leah endured her father's rejection and shame was by imagining that someday, some way, God would bring a man into her life who would love her. However, tonight Satan will lock her into the destiny of never knowing a man's love, either in the form of a father or a husband.

When the marriage feasting peaks, the bridegroom is led to his tent in celebration, and the marriage is consummated. And that night, the bride lays beside her deceived husband silently weeping tears of shame, for all of her fondest dreams were crushed under the shame of her own deception. From the time she had been a child and played wedding, she had imagined what it would be like to be the bride, and now that dream was crushed. She had committed spiritual suicide.

She cried herself to sleep, much like the night Jacob cried himself to sleep. The difference was that that on this night there would be no dream. It would be delayed, and the nightmare would intensify before the Father's blessing would be revealed. The morning dawns, and the lifted veil lies crumpled above the bed, the light reveals the face of Leah, the eyes of Jacob are shocked with unbelief, and his scream penetrates the morning silence. "It's Leah!" he shouts, and bursts from the tent to find Laban.

He has been deceived. Two emotions, guilt and anger, vie for supremacy. Guilt. accompanied by irony, replays his own deception. Anger over being deceived seeks revenge. Adrenaline courses through his veins as he confronts Laban. "IT'S LEAH! WHERE IS RACHEL?" Laban's response is unbelievable. He says, "It's not the practice in our place to marry off the younger before the firstborn."

Don't you hate policy responses? That's exactly what Laban gave. It's not our policy around here in this neighborhood.

"BUT WHAT ABOUT YOUR PROMISE, LABAN?"

"Well, I tell you what. You complete the wedding week with Leah, and we'll have another wedding next week, and then you can work seven more years, and we'll call it all square."

The dialogue must have been very heated. Accusations must have flown. Faces were red and nerves were raw, but in the final analysis, Laban's solution was the one accepted. And the next week, Jacob married Rachel, and Leah's life struck rock bottom. For you see, the only time that Leah knew what it was like to be loved by a man was the night she dressed up like her sister. And the only time Jacob knew what it was like to be loved by his father was the day he dressed up like his brother.

These two children of shame, these two deprived of the blessing, were now brought together in marriage. The lack of self-worth in their lives was magnified by their marriage.

All too often, people who have not been blessed hope that marriage will be the turning point and the time of blessing. But unless both mates are filled with the blessing of a heavenly Father, they will not have enough to overflow in affirmation to one another.

But now the heavenly Father steps onto the scene, not with the sudden burst of a dream but with the continuous affirmation of childbearing. The greatest evidence of a wife's value was her ability to bear children, and the children of greatest value were males. Scripture records, "Now the Lord saw that Leah was unloved, and He opened her womb, but Rachel's was barren." God intentionally brings Leah to the attention of her peers—this is her moment. For the first time in her life, friends and neighbors would call her blessed. He removes Rachel from center stage. The Father loves to bless the unloved. It pains Him to see His children's worth diminished, and He longs to restore with divine blessing the scars of human shame.

God began to manifest His blessing on Leah, and for the first time, a father figure stepped into her life with affirmation. And Leah conceived. For the first time in her life, people bega to affirm her. Women called her blessed. When the child was born, she named him Reuben.

The name Reuben reveals how deep the pain of shame can be, for when your earthly father doesn't love you and your husband doesn't love you, it is difficult to believe that the heavenly Father loves you. God is trying to get through to Leah by giving her children. But she names the baby out of her shame, not His blessing. "Look—a son. Now won't you love me?" is the meaning of the name Reuben.

She conceives again the second year of their marriage—the second year when Rachel is barren. The second year when the women are heaping praise on Leah and pity on Rachel. But Leah still cannot hear the blessing of God through the gift of children. When this child is born, she names him Simeon.

Two children, two boys, two great blessings, eighteen months of knowing the power of God's gift alive in you—but the pain still shackles her to the shame. Simeon means, "God has heard that I am unloved, and He has given me a son."

The third year, the scenario is the same. Rachel is barren. Leah is fertile. God's blessing is again bestowed on Leah. This time she again has a son. Three years, three sons. She names him Levi, which means, "Now perhaps this time my husband will become attached to me." She hopes that the third time will be a charm to Jacob. Three boys. What more could a man ask? This will surely win his love. Wrong!

Year four, and she becomes pregnant again. Year four, and Rachel is still barren. Year four, and Leah finally begins to realize that this is a sign that God values her. The neighborhood is buzzing. "Leah is so blessed. Look—three sons! Jacob should be proud." The fourth son is born, and God's Sabbath blessing breaks through to Leah's shame. She names him Judah, which means, "Praise the Lord."

> "They looked to Him and were radiant, and their faces shall never be ashamed."
> —Psalm 34:5.

Forget Jacob, forget Laban—remember the heavenly Father. In the birth of Judah, Leah realizes the blessing of her Father. In the birth of Judah comes the moment for Leah when she sees the dream of her worth in God's eyes. In the birth of Judah she is set free from the prison of people pleasing. Leah is through with looking to people for affirmation. Three years of hoping that this baby would win Jacob's love have been met with the crushing disappointment of the same old Jacob. The reality is that he may never change, and it is painful, but no longer her soul source of worth. For she has finally realized that she has a heavenly Father's affirmation—and that will be her strength. Judah is to Leah what Bethel was to Jacob. The birth of Judah is the point at which the Father's blessing breaks through and she is reborn into a heavenly family. For Jacob it was a dream—for Leah it was a baby.

As she cradled the baby in her arms, she felt the warmth of the Father's blessing and love surrounding both mother and child. For the first time she visualized God smiling at her and felt like a favorite child. Her heart seemed to burst with joy, and she decided to memorialize the moment by naming the baby Judah. It was the end of the names of shame and the beginning of the names of blessing.

And I believe this is why God chooses Judah to be the father of the Messiah. Christ's parenting comes not through the traditional genealogy of the firstborn, but it through son number four, Judah, because this is the son of blessing.

This is the moment of blessing for Leah. This is the moment of original love in her life. Love deprived now gives way to love realized. Sabbath has brought both life and meaning, and Leah is redefined as blessed.

Judah was the line of the Messiah, because in the birth of Judah there was the rebirth of Leah, as she found her true Father in heaven. The Bible punctuates this with biology, for it says that Leah now stopped bearing children. It was also characterized by a new day for Leah, for the scripture says, "Now when Rachel saw that she bore Jacob no children, she became jealous of her sister." No one had ever been jealous of Leah in her life. They had always felt sorry for her, but they had never been jealous of her until God filled her life with the blessing of children and filled her heart with the blessing of the heavenly Father. Then, for the first time, she had something that someone wanted. Jealousy was the final proof that she had regained her worth. Rachel has never wanted to be Leah until now. Praise the Lord, Leah is finally free from her sister's pity.

"And [Rachel] said to Jacob, 'Give me children or else I die.' And Jacob's anger burned against Rachel, and he said, 'Am I in the place of God, who has withheld from you the fruit of the womb?'"

It was clearly understood that God was blessing Leah. Now God stops, as if to say, "Rest, Leah. Savor the reality I have just given you—that you have finally heard that I love you."

This message is difficult to hear when the voices around you tell you that you are not worthy of any love. Rachel will not have children until Leah's time of childbearing is complete. But now, God wants Leah to rest and drink in the blessing before her childbearing resumes. She needs to absorb the miracle that has taken place in her life and the meaning of being blessed. She needs it to redeem the past and reinforce the present, for the future will not be easy. Just because she has experienced the affirmation of God does not mean that the rejection of men will be easy to bear.

In time, the rest is over, and childbearing resumes as Leah gives birth to her fifth son, Issachar, which means, "God has given me my reward."

Leah conceives her sixth son and decides to name him Zebulun, which can be translated, "My husband will honor, or bless, me because I have born him six sons." In the naming of Zebulun, Leah reveals that she still longs to be blessed by her husband, yet we have no record that such blessing and honor ever occurred.

The heritage of Leah is that she brought the blessing to her children without the assistance of a husband, and those children went on to make up half the tribes of God's chosen people. She is the model for women who are single parents. Leah reveals the goodness of God and the cruelty of man.

The most incredible part of this story is that Leah learned to live without the love of an earthly father or husband. This was made possible because she was reparented by a heavenly Father, who enabled her to live the blessing in a land of cursing. God kept reaffirming her with the greatest responsibility He could ever give to any human being, which is to raise a child filled with worth and value. Six times He gives her the gift of life to imbue with blessing.

Now, to make her life complete, the Jewish proverb says that she should have seven sons. God blesses Leah a seventh time, and she becomes pregnant. But this is one of God's wonderful twists to human expectation. This baby is a girl, and I believe that God was saying, "Leah, you have heard now that you are loved. Now I entrust to you the spirit of a woman to fill her with a mother's affirmation, to turn her face to a heavenly Father and fill her full and make her new. Bring all the blessing to her that you never had in your life."

And I believe that Leah heard the message, because she named her baby Dinah, which means, "God is my judge." Take the judgment of no man—your father, or husband, or any man—for your worth is not theirs to determine. God is your Judge, and He will bless you with the power of original love to flow into your spirit and give you worth. At the birth of Judah, Leah begins to live the blessing. At the birth of Dinah, the blessing is completed. The seventh child is the complete recognition of God as the source of blessing, and she expresses it in the name Dinah. She will turn this child's face toward the heavenly Father and teach her that her worth can never be subject to the judgment of another. As God completes His work with Sabbath, Leah completes her life-giving work by memorializing the blessing of Sabbath.

The beauty of this story is that Dinah, herself, was so beautiful that a prince wanted to marry her. The tragedy of the story is that he misused her, and she was a victim of rape—the action of a man would fill her life with shame. How did she endure? The only answer I find plausible is that she drew from the spiritual heritage of her mother, who taught her that she had a heavenly Father who could fill her with worth that would enable her to live beyond the shame of human experience.

The Gospel according to Leah is the power of God's blessing. It is so important that He punctuated its saving power by having the Messiah come to earth as the son of Judah. Baby Judah brought Sabbath blessing to a woman shamed. Jesus the "Lion of the tribe of Judah" brought Sabbath blessing to a world shamed.

Leah's life stands as a witness to the power of Sabbath blessing. It is still true today. If as a child you knew the pain of shame, you need to know the power of Sabbath blessing. God's plan is for each baby to be parented by an earthly father who would bless his child and introduce him or her to the Sabbath blessing of the heavenly Father. But in a world of shame, the devil smiles as unblessed children wander the face of the earth crying out for love. The Father calls these children to "look up" to Him and receive the Sabbath blessing.

When I meet any of these children, my heart is broken. Their stories fill me with sadness. But I tell them the story of Jacob and Leah, two unloved children whose lives were changed by the power of the blessing. I tell them that I cannot change their earthly father, but I can introduce them to a heavenly Father who offers them the opportunity to be born again. This rebirth will make them part of the heavenly family, and each Sabbath they can come to the Father's house, where He will bless them over and over again.

If you need to experience the Sabbath Blessing through rebirth, you can meet with God's earthly family and create a new home right here, right now, called church. It is the only solution that I know that really works. And it's FREE from the Father, with love. Every Sabbath He still walks through our earth to bless His children.

Have you received the blessing?

19

Living the Blessing in the Land of Cursing

"THEN THE LORD SAID to Jacob, return to the land of your fathers and to your relatives, and I will be with you. I am the God of Bethel, where you anointed a pillar, where you made a vow to me. Now arise, leave this land and return to the land of your birth."

Why would God send Jacob home?

His mother had died. The only person who loved him was gone. His father never really loved him, and Esau, his brother, was waiting to kill him. It was a place where his name was a byword. Where, around the campfires when they wanted to describe a person in the worst possible way, they said he was a "Jacob."

Why go home? It would only open old wounds and subject his entire family to all the sordid history of his shameful past. Sometimes you must go back to go forward. You must deal with the mistakes you have made, and you must look into the eyes of those who have rejected you and find that God's blessing has the power to help you go beyond the past.

So Jacob starts the journey back. It is as if God knows that He is sending Jacob into the teeth of a storm of shame, where all his personal history will wash over him.

To enable Jacob to make the journey, God meets him at critical points along the road home to reinforce the blessing. "Now as Jacob went on his way, the angels of God met him, and Jacob said when he saw them, 'This is God's camp.'" It is as if God is leading Jacob down His "yellow ribbon" road, reminding him that he is of eternal worth.

As Jacob sees the angels, he experiences a flashback to Bethel. The feelings were the same, but the direction was different. He was running away from home then, but now he is returning. The angels were connecting him with his Heavenly Father then. Now they gather around him to protect him from his earthly brother. They move with the precision of an omnipotent army, dividing into two groups. One positions itself in the front and the other in the back.

Can you imagine the calm that would settle over you if you were Jacob? You know full well that your brother is aware of your return—no doubt Laban has attended to that matter. You cannot sleep for fear of an ambush.

Then suddenly as night settles and fears peak, an angel army appears. Rest floods your spirit, and fear is replaced by the security of guardian angels. It is heaven's night light in Jacob's dark and frightening world. The psalmist will memorialize this story with the words, "He will give His angels charge over thee to guard you in all your ways."

Sometimes you must hear heaven in order to live on earth! When your inner world is barren and your outer world is hostile, God subdues the torment with blessing.

Buying Blessing

The next morning Jacob decides to make a gesture of reconciliation to his brother Esau. Jacob exhibits the deep need in the human spirit for acceptance and affirmation.

In our efforts, we often make ourselves vulnerable to the actions of those who would crush our spirit. Jacob sends the messengers out with this charge: "Thus you shall say to my lord Esau. Thus says your servant Jacob, I have sojourned with Laban and stayed until now, and I have oxen and donkeys and flocks and male and female servants, and I have sent to tell my lord that I might find favor [blessing] in your sight."

The vulnerability of Jacob is that he is always looking for blessing from the people around him, and they always disappoint him.

Notice the three ploys:

1. He builds Esau up as the one of greatest worth by calling him "my lord."

2. He subjects himself by referring to himself as "your servant."

3. He seeks to buy favor with gifts.

But none of these attempts work. The messengers return and give their report. "We came to your brother Esau, and, furthermore, he is coming to meet you with 400 men are with him." Esau dashes his hope for acceptance just as he had dashed the hopes of Leah. But he will try again.

Jacob's next response is to send gifts of cattle and livestock from his possessions to Esau. And as he sends those gifts, he gives the servants a message to deliver.

"Behold your servant Jacob is also behind us, for he said, I will appease him with the present that goes before me and then afterwards I will see his face and perhaps he will accept me." Jacob lowers his expectations from affirmation to appeasement.

Sin always seeks to put you down, and when you are vulnerable, it seeks to completely terrorize you. When you are weak, it seeks to prey on your spirit, to take every energy away from you. Jacob is afraid and discouraged. One of my father's favorite sayings is, "Discouragement is the devil's anesthesia, when he wants to take your heart out."

Jacob's quest in life is the blessing of men. The tragedy is that humans shame him, but the glory is that God blesses him.

Jacob turns his hope for favor and rescue to the Lord. He crosses over the brook Jabbok to pray. But upon arriving on the other side, he is ambushed unexpectedly by a man, and they engage in hand-to-hand combat. Jacob does not know that he is wrestling with God until the Lord touches his hip and dislocates it. "And the Lord says, 'Let Me go, for the dawn is breaking,' but Jacob says, 'I will not let you go unless you bless me.'"

For the second time, he meets God in the hour of his darkest need. For the second time, God breaks through with blessing. But this time the blessing goes all the way back to his first point of shame, as God asks him, "What is your name?" And he said, "Jacob." And God said, "Your name shall no longer be Jacob, but Israel." In Bethel the Father's blessing enabled Jacob to shape his future. Tonight at Jabbok, the Father's blessing will redeem his past.

Yes, the Father who blessed him when he was homeless would give him a new name. God knew the power that the past can have on a life. God's new name released him from his old name and his old shame. No doubt others would continue to call him Jacob, and the venom of vengeance would seep through the syllables. It is hard to endure the names others call you, but it is possible when God has given you a new name.

Do you need a new name? Scripture says that in heaven you will receive a new name. One of the best ways to embed original love into your life today is to hear heaven's name. Call yourself that name and discard all others, for heaven's name is your hope to live the blessing in the land of cursing.

And the Bible says, "Your name shall no longer be Jacob, but Israel."

What is your name? List them all, and then select a name of heaven's blessing, insert a new name, and hear God say, "You shall no longer be called by those old names of shame, but you shall be called by the new name of blessing."

For Jacob, this was like a runner, facing the point of exhaustion and receiving a second wind. Suddenly the second wind comes in the second blessing, and Jacob, in turn, renames this place. Just as he renamed Luz to Bethel, he renames Jabbok to Penuel, "For he said, I have seen God face to face, and yet my life has been preserved."

The scripture account is not only factual in that it describes the dawn, but also symbolic in that it captures the experience—as it says, "Now the sun rose upon him just as he crossed over Penuel, and he was limping on his thigh."

When you hear heaven's name, you can go into the land of cursing knowing that you carry the power of the blessing and that truly the Son has risen upon you. Although Jacob was disabled in his body, he was enabled in his spirit. He was less equipped to face Esau physically, but he was mightily equipped to face him spiritually. And Jacob lifts up his eyes and sees Esau with his 400 men. He walks toward him with a noticeable limp, bowing seven times before he reaches them, and somehow, Esau has been changed. He embraces Jacob and kisses him, and they weep together.

Esau looks around and is amazed by all the gifts and all the wealth that Jacob has accrued, and he asks, "What do you mean by all this company which I have met?" And Jacob responds, "To find favor in the sight of my Lord." He is still seeking to purchase human favor.

And Esau says, "I have plenty, my brother, let what you have be your own." And Jacob says, "No, please, if now I have found favor in your sight, then take my presents from my hand."

The miracle of the blessing is that it changes the way you see even your worst critics and those who put you down. It changes the way you talk to yourself. It changes the way you think of yourself. Here Jacob reveals how the blessing has transformed his picture of Esau, for he says, "I see your face as one sees the face of God."

When God has smiled upon you and let you know that you are a prince, a child of the King, you can take the power of that smile and transfer it to your worst critic.

Jacob has been reborn by a heavenly Father who blesses him with a new name. He has given him a new home—Bethel—and a new name—Israel. He has given him a new perspective on an older brother. And He longs to do the same for every child who has been shamed. Each Sabbath He looks down upon you, waiting for you to look up and receive the blessing. And for all who will stop and look up, He promises that "They will look to Him and become radiant, and their faces will never be ashamed"!

Experiencing
Sabbath Blessing

SABBATH BLESSING ... to experience the abundant affirmation and favor of God on the Sabbath day and instill a sense of identity and belonging.

Examples of ways to experience the Sabbath Blessing on Sabbath and throughout the week:

1. Every Sabbath, in the Jewish tradition, Des, as the spiritual leader of our home, gives a personalized Sabbath blessing to each member of the family. The Sabbath blessing has three components:

• A meaningful touch.

• Words of affirmation for a positive future (usually a scripture).

• His personal commitment to the individual toward fulfilling that future.

This blessing is usually given on Friday evening or on a Sabbath morning.

2. For over ten years, every Sabbath breakfast, along with the special Sabbath pitcher for milk or juice and traditional muffins, we have a variety of beautiful paper napkins on which we write the person's name and words of affirmation—using our imagination and creativity.

3. Every year, we celebrate each family member's spiritual birthday—first with their dedication day and then their baptism day. Since we love celebrating birthdays and other special occasions, we desire to put equal energy and emphasis into celebrating our eternal birthday. We celebrate these on the Sabbath closest to the baptismal date. We have a party—decorations and all! We buy the person some new clothing, and invite relatives and friends for the meal of their personally selected menu. Along with the gifts to them, we give a special thank offering for them at church.

4. Our family has a commitment to pray for each other at 12 noon each day—Des even sets his watch alarm to remind him. This has been a really affirming connection that we share.

5. Many times we use the Sabbath hours to write notes to each other and/or to relatives/friends. "You are/were a blessing to me when you_____."

6. One holiday that we use for blessing is Thanksgiving. We have a three-foot white painted tree branch that we call our Thanksgiving Tree. We have different colors of paper cut like leaves, and each person writes not only about what they are thankful for in life but also about each other person.

7. Every since our children were small, we have used a Bible character to affirm them and to show that they are favored by God. For example:

"Derek, you reminded me of David when you played your violin."

"Tracy, you reminded me of Esther, the shining star, today when you were true to your belief and principles."

"Derek, I saw some of Joseph in you today when you were building your fort. You have good building skills."

"Tracy, I saw qualities of Dorcas in you today when you helped Mrs. Allen."

8. We have a special Affirmation Plate that we use at a mealtime for any special accomplishments or unselfish acts: good grades, a recital, a spontaneous act of kindness, and so on.

Some ways to extend the blessing to other people:

1. For new neighbors, during the week we bake a small loaf of bread and take it to them on Sabbath to welcome them to their new home and to our neighborhood. A small loaf of bread or muffins means so much to caregivers or members of a family in which someone is ill or has had surgery.

2. For church youth attending a school out of the town, we make care packages to send to them with special notes or texts of blessing or affirmation.

For other ideas and sharing, visit our Website: *originalove.com.*

The Journey to Sanctification

20

A Family Divided

WHEN LEAH STOPPED giving birth, God opened the womb of Rachel, and she became pregnant. The dynamic of the family changed immediately. Leah's sons carried the pain of their mother's quest for the love of her husband. Their names spoke of her unmet need. Their numbers alone should have called for some reward, but it was clear that Jacob's heart would not let go of the anger over her deception. He would punish her for the past.

When Rachel gave birth to a son, she named him Joseph, which means; "may God add." The name revealed the underlying competition between the two sisters. The implication is that Rachel wanted God to continue to gift her with sons, that she might catch up with Leah in the nation-building race. She wanted to mother as many tribes as Leah. She believed the prophecy of a great nation, and she understood that each of Jacob's sons would be the father of a tribe. She wanted to leave her legacy of sons, and she wanted them to be the most favored.

The eleven sons of Jacob formed a dysfunctional family. Eight came from Leah and her maid. Three came from Rachel and her maid. Their mothers were at war with each other. Their jealousy and contention flared often within the family, and the birth of Joseph compounded the situation.

It is almost incomprehensible that Jacob, who knew the devastating impact of favoritism, would perpetuate it within his own family. But that's exactly what he did, and when Joseph turned 17 years of age, Jacob sent him out to work the flocks with his brothers. He had already sheltered him too long.

A shepherd boy would typically begin his work at an earlier age—perhaps 12, not 17. Jacob had exempted his favorite son from manual labor. But finally he is sent out with his brothers and returns home with a bad report. Apparently his brothers had done something he did not approve of, and he told his father.

Jacob responded by rewarding him with a coat of many colors. The scripture says, "Now Israel loved Joseph more than all of his sons, because he was the son of his old age, and he made him a varied colored tunic. And his brothers saw that their father loved him more than all his brothers, and so they hated him and could not speak to him on friendly terms."

What's so bad about a coat of many colors?

Simply this: It had long sleeves, and it carried a message in the symbol of the long sleeves. For, you see, only princes wore a tunic with long sleeves. Common workers wore a sleeveless tunic so that they could get down to their tasks. When Jacob gave Joseph a long-sleeved coat, he in effect said, "This is the prince of the family. He is the one who will rule over all of you, and he will carry my name. No matter where the rest of you are in the birth order, I have redrawn the will, and it starts with Joseph."

Can you imagine the dinner table? It would have been a place where sarcasm, criticism, and bitterness were perpetuated by cold glances and sharp words. It was a cold war that Jacob allowed and even incited. And as if that wasn't enough, Joseph had a dream. The dream's origin was from God, but the telling of the dream created an ungodly impact on the brothers.

Imagine the setting after a hard workday. The family gathers around the dinner fires, and as they finish their meal, Joseph speaks up. "Please listen to this dream which I had. For behold, we were binding sheaths in the field, and my sheath stood up and also stood erect and, behold, your sheaves gathered around and bowed down to my sheath."

Then his brothers said, "Are you actually going to reign over us? Are you really going to rule over us?" So they hated him even more for his dreams and his words.

"Then he had a second dream, and he related it to his brothers, saying, 'I had still another dream, and behold, the sun and the moon and the eleven stars are bowing down to me.' And he related it to his father and to his brothers, and his father rebuked him and said, 'What is this dream that you have had? Shall I and your mother and your brothers actually come to bow ourselves down before you to the ground?' And his father was jealous of him, but his father kept the saying in mind."

Apparently, Jacob's rebuke was anything but effective, for he obviously didn't truly act in a convincing way. But in a symbolic way he chided his son while enjoying the dream himself and keeping it in his mind. And the brothers, sensing this, added malice to hatred.

This state of things must have been most difficult for the sons of Leah, especially for Reuben, the firstborn, who according to tradition, was the one who should receive the inheritance—the one who should be the leader of the family. But the noticeable absence of their brother Joseph with the flocks and the noticeable presence of his coat of many colors so fractured their family that a cold war set in—a war of words, short tempers, and threats.

The flocks and herds had to be moved to find pastureland, so distance was put between the home camp and the working camp of the brothers. "It came about that Israel said to Joseph, 'Are not your brothers pasturing the flock in Shechem? Come, and I will send you to them.' And he said to him, 'I will go.'"

Jacob's lack of understanding about what was going on in his own family, combined with his favoritism, created the backdrop for violence to break out.

It is unbelievable that a father would be so naive as to take this kind of action—to send out a son who was his favorite, who he knew the brothers resented and hated, to visit them, dressed in his coat of many colors with its symbolic meaning.

It is incomprehensible that he did not understand the risks, unless he thought that this was the moment the young prince should go out and inspect his brothers and, in fact, begin to exercise the first signs of his family leadership.

It is incomprehensible that Joseph did not understand how his coming to see his brothers dressed in the coat of many colors would only incite more hatred. He must have had other coats he could have worn. It is certain that he had a work coat—one without the long sleeves— a coat that would signal that he had come to help, not to inspect. He must have known what their reaction would be, and he must have enjoyed the thought enough to choose to wear the coat.

And, the Bible says, "When they saw him from a distance, before he came close, they plotted against him to put him to death. And they said to one another, 'Here comes this dreamer. Now come, let's kill him and throw him into one of the pits, and we will say a wild beast devoured him, and then let us see what will become of his dreams.'"

When a family becomes dysfunctional, it can be traced to many factors, but the common symptom is violence, whether it is verbal or physical—the steadied understanding of the temperament of each member is orchestrated by hatred, manifest by abuse, leading to violence.

Can you relate to this type of family?

Reuben, the firstborn, who has the most to gain from Joseph's death, intervenes and suggests, "Let us not take his life. Shed no blood, but throw him into this pit in the wilderness." His plan was to come back later and rescue him. They tear off Joseph's tunic, and amidst his pleadings for mercy, they throw him into a pit.

The venom of hatred spews over into language that colors the air. This is not the fulfillment of a dream but the beginning of a nightmare of family violence. Reuben's pleadings end the beating of their brother, and they sit down to eat, accompanied by groaning from the pit. While they are eating, a caravan appears on the horizon, and Judah has a bright idea. "Let's sell him to the Ishmaelites. It doesn't really profit us to kill our brother, but we could make some money and deal with this problem by making him a slave." So they sold him for twenty shekels of silver.

Can you imagine it? Selling your brother into slavery and selling him to the family's worst enemy, the Ishmaelites? Guaranteed abuse, all the way to Egypt! Joseph would be the target of every slur Ishmael had ever dreamed up to throw at Isaac, for he had passed the hatred down in the form of prejudice. The child of works is now in control of the family of promise.

Joseph's sanctifying moment came as the caravan passed the tents of his father on the way to Egypt. As the view of the tents disappeared Joseph must have felt an overwhelming sense of separation from his father Israel. The realization that this may be his last glimpse of home must have been accompanied by the despair of loneliness. Broken in body and spirit, he could have been overcome by sorrow. But from the depths of his pain he reaches toward heaven and asks God to walk with him through the shadows of his life. He gives himself totally to the God of his father. Unlike Abraham, Joseph entered Egypt set apart by God for a holy purpose.

Have you experienced sanctification?

21

Human Wrongs

JOSEPH'S EARLY LIFE was filled with the ongoing impact of original sin. All the dysfunctional elements of blame that separate people seemed to be manifest in his life.

His dysfunctional family erupts in violence and abuse, and he is sold into slavery. Society, instead of providing him with his human rights, deprives him of dignity, and he is subjected to the slave market.

Twice sold—first by his own brothers, and second by the enemies of his family, the Ishmaelites—Joseph now sits enslaved in Egypt, the kingdom of darkness. From the slave market he is sold again to Potiphar, the captain of Pharaoh's guard. From this pit of human slavery, he is taken into one of the most elite households of the community. Because the Lord has given him abundant talent, everything he touches prospers. For the first time since his father's house, he begins to find a place where he is welcomed.

In fact, he is made overseer of the entire house, and everything seems to be going well. Unfortunately, original sin is not through with him yet. He will experience the fractures of the workplace, starting with sexual harassment. For you see, Joseph was handsome, and the master's wife looked at him with desire and tried to seduce him. This apparently went on for some time, but Joseph's answer was always the same: "How can I do this great evil and sin against God?"

Through careful planning, Potiphar's wife set up a situation where she could be alone with Joseph, and when she threw herself at him, he fled, and she grabbed his garment. Her desire turned to resentment, anger, and revenge. No slave would get away with rejecting her. If she allowed this to happen, she would never have the respect of her servants. If he had only been smart enough to play the game, he could have had everything he wanted, but now she will punish him.

With his cloak in her hand, she called to the men of the household and said to them, "See, Potiphar has brought in a Hebrew to us to make sport of us, and he came in to lie with me, and I screamed, and he ran away and left his garment as he fled."

How easy it would have been for Joseph to just act like a slave and play the role Potiphar's wife wanted him to. Such an action might even have been common and accepted. But circumstances are never more powerful than one's commitment—and Joseph's very identity was determined by his commitment. He was given to God—set apart for a holy use.

Instead of being conformed by the culture around him, Joseph chose to be transformed by the Spirit. But when you refuse to play the devil's game, he tries to break you with his most powerful tools: seduction, harassment, racism, injustice, slavery, and prejudice.

Racism was the second tool of human blame that Potiphar's wife chose to inflict upon Joseph with the negative impact of a fractured workplace. When Potiphar came home, she spoke to him with the same prejudice: "The Hebrew slave whom you bought for us came in to make sport of me, and it happened as I raised my voice and screamed, that he left his garment beside me and fled."

The prejudice against the Hebrews traced back to Abraham's visit to Egypt, when God had delivered him with wealth and punished

Pharaoh's household with barrenness. Racial prejudice is a powerful thing that seems to strengthen over generations, so Potiphar was angry with Joseph and put him into the king's prison.

Have you ever been hurt by racism?

He must have had an inkling about the character of his wife, for instead of killing Joseph, he put him in prison. And instead of putting him into the worst prison, he put him into the prison where the king's prisoners were confined.

Look at Joseph's plight. Just as he was starting to make progress, sexual harassment and prejudice fractured his work environment. The courts, manipulated by the elite, administered injustice, and he was thrust into the pits again. Isn't this the moment to give up on God? Isn't this the time to admit that right does not make might? In fact, the opposite seems true—"might makes right." Isn't it time to get smart and play the power game—to go it alone? Not if you're sanctified—not if you're Joseph.

It isn't long before Joseph begins to be noticed by the head jailer. Joseph makes his progress to leadership in that environment, and one day, two officials are thrown into prison: the chief cupbearer and the chief baker. They each have a dream.

Now, it would seem by this time Joseph would be disillusioned about interpreting dreams, but when he found these men dejected and discouraged about the meaning of their dream, he interpreted them both. To one, he prophesied his death—the baker. To the other, he prophesied his release—the cupbearer. And when he was released, Joseph asked him but one favor—to remember him. He said, "Keep me in mind when it goes well with you. Please do me a kindness by mentioning me to Pharaoh, and get me out of this house, for I was, in fact, kidnapped from the land of the Hebrews, and even here I have done nothing that would have put me into the dungeon."

Enduring injustice is one of the most difficult challenges of life, especially when that injustice occurs with the regularity of daily work. For Joseph, two years passed. Two years in which injustice was perpetuated in the prison of Pharaoh. Two years in which hope faded and the realization that he was forgotten had the opportunity to breed bitterness.

Has injustice affected your life?

If you have ever wondered when the record would be set straight for you, yet it seems to linger, you know what Joseph was going through. A victim of family violence, slavery, harassment, racism, and injustice, Joseph knew all of the brokenness of life. Surely this would create the bedrock of bitterness and the rage of revenge. This is the profile of many a serial killer and tyrant.

How can Sanctification heal a life this broken?

22

New Beginnings

ALTARS MARKED THE GREAT MOMENTS in Abraham's life. The great moments in Joseph's life were marked by dreams.

When humans are at their worst, God draws close to heal the brokenness of a blame-based society, and it begins in Pharaoh's bedroom, as God gives him two dreams. One dream features fat cows and thin cows. The second dream brings to view fat, plump ears of corn and thin, skinny, wind-scorched ears of corn.

Both dreams end with the horrific scene of the thin eating the fat. They were dreams to remember. Dream that were disturbing. Dreams that baffled the magicians of Egypt. But when they reached the ears of the cupbearer, they were like a wake-up call.

He told Pharaoh of the Hebrew prisoner who had been able to interpret his dream. "And Pharaoh sent and called for Joseph, who interpreted the dream, and when he was finished gave the counsel to Pharaoh that he should take action to appoint overseers in charge of the land and let them exact one-fifth of the produce of the land of Egypt in the seven years of abundance.

"'Let them gather all the food of these good years that are coming, and store up the grain for food in the cities under Pharaoh's authority and let them guard it, and let the food become as a reserve for the land for the seven years of famine which will occur in the land of Egypt, so that the land may not perish during the famine.'

"Now this proposal seemed good to Pharaoh and to all of his servants. And then Pharaoh said to his servants, 'Can we find a man like this in whom there is a divine spirit?'"

Joseph had made it plain that God was the source of his interpretation and wisdom, and Pharaoh said, "'Since God has informed you of all this, there is no one so discerning and wise as you. You shall be over my house, and according to your command, all my people shall do homage. Only in the throne I will be greater than you.' And he offered him his signet ring and clothed him in garments of fine linen and put a gold necklace around his neck, and he had him ride his second chariot, and they proclaimed it throughout the land."

And Pharaoh named him Zaphenath-paneah, which means, "What God says, He does." The Egyptian name recognized that Joseph was sanctified. Within a few short hours, through divine action, injustice was replaced by privilege, racism by rights, and harassment by honor. God was beginning to put Joseph's outer world back together, beginning first with his work life. But the true power of Joseph's life was the commitment of his inner world to God despite the circumstances of his outer world.

Pharaoh took a second action. "Then Pharaoh gave him Asenath, the daughter of Potiphar, the priest of On, as his wife. And Joseph was thirty years old."

Thirteen years had passed since his family had rejected him, abused him, and sold him into slavery. Now God was going to establish His own family.

The foundation of unity is established in the family. It was true at creation. It was true with Joseph, and it is true in the twenty-first century. Even in the midst of Egypt, God provided him with a woman who could join him in creating a home united by spiritual values and characterized by sanctification.

Our knowledge of Asenath is limited, yet the greatest evidence of the unity of their marriage is expressed in the birth of their two sons and the names they chose for each. Joseph named the firstborn Manasseh. The meaning of that name is, "God has made me forget all my trouble in my father's household." This would imply that the quality of his family life with Asenath was filled with such love that he was able to start again. His relationship with God and his wife made it possible for him to forget the past.

Do you have issues in your life you want to forget?

If you have been injured or mistreated by your family or in your workplace, the first healing God would give you is the ability to forget all those who have troubled you and hurt you deeply—to offer them forgiveness as He did when He prayed from the cross, "Father, forgive them, for they know not what they do."

Joseph not only had his family to forgive, he also had Potiphar's wife to forgive and forget. The greatest test for a person who has been mistreated, when they come to power, is to misuse that power to get revenge on the enemies.

Joseph's struggle on the road of sanctification is the struggle between forgiveness and revenge. So many people who have been hurt by others are unable to move beyond being controlled by the same people who have hurt them. You can't talk with them for more than five minutes before they are compelled to tell you their story. They graphically explain how they have been mistreated. Their anger stirs as they recite all of the injustices. They seem to be locked in the prison of self-nurtured memories as victims of bitterness.

Do you have people to forgive and wrongs to forget?

Bitterness is the inability to forgive someone who has hurt you so that you can go forward. It is walking backward into the future with your eyes fixed on those who have hurt you in the past, thus setting you up to fall backward into the future.

It has been said that we would do well to chart our lives after the law of the windshield and mirror. Every car is required by law to be equipped with a windshield and a rearview mirror. The windshield is for looking forward and the mirror for looking back. The rearview mirror is one-hundredth the size of the windshield, implying that 99 percent of the time, you need to be looking forward. Imagine how many accidents would occur if this were reversed. You would be forced to have 99 percent of your visual field filled with views of the past and only 1 percent available for looking forward. It would have a paralyzing effect on your driving.

This is exactly the situation for the person who is shackled to the past. Such people feel they have no future because of the tragedies of their past.

When you experience the forgiveness of God, you can extend it to others. It is not natural, but by the grace of God, it is supernatural. It will reframe your past and free you from its paralyzing power. Every once in a while, memory will call you to look back, but by the grace of God, as you glance back, you will see a different history. Through the forgiving power of the cross, you can let go of those things that would capture your spirit and plunge it into bitterness—those things you cannot change but that can hold you captive.

Have you experienced the blessing of Manasseh?

Manasseh sets the stage for God's second gift of sanctification—Ephraim, "the ability to be fruitful in the land of my affliction." Who would have dreamed that a Hebrew slave could have become prime minister of Egypt? Through unity with God, you will be empowered to demonstrate God's greatest gifts at the point of your deepest hurt. Sabbath will sanctify your suffering and transform your troubles. United with God, you can grow the fruit of love in the land of pain.

Has God given you the gift of Ephraim?

Ephraim follows Manasseh as Pentecost follows the cross. In fact, the burning question of the disciples to those who had received the forgiveness of the cross, symbolized by baptism, was, "Have you received the Spirit?" The beauty of God's plan for sanctifying your life is that He offers to take away your past and transform your present so that together, you may create a future. God is not about turning the negatives in your life to zero, He is about transforming them into positives.

The cross and the Spirit! Manassah represents the power of the cross, and Ephraim the power of the Spirit. God's key to unlock the doors of the prison of the past is forgiveness. And His key to turn your tragedy to triumph is the sanctifying Spirit.

Wait just a minute! Joseph is an example of how God sanctifies righteous people who are hurt by a wicked world. But the real question is, "Does sanctification work for people who bring brokenness on themselves?"

The answer resides at Calvary. A thief hangs on the cross next to Jesus. He has brought this suffering on himself. Yet as he watches Jesus, he is drawn to Him, and as he hears Jesus pray for the crowd, he cries out, "Lord, remember me!" Sanctifying power has awakened his desire to be with Jesus, and the Lord responds without hesitation, "You will be with Me in Paradise." Sanctification longs to forgive and forget. Sanctifying love always seeks to mend the broken with forgiveness and turn the deserved cross into an undeserved crown. And it is never too late!

23

Making a Nation Great

WHY WOULD GOD REINTRODUCE Joseph to the pain of the past? Apparently Joseph had no desire to discover what was happening with his family, for seven years of plenty had passed. It gave him the time in which he could have easily found out about his family's well-being, sent them a warning message that a famine was on its way, or made a personal visit, but none of these had taken place.

Perhaps the reason is that when you have been abused at home, your greatest quest is simply to forget it and never bring it to mind. Apparently this was the case with Joseph. He was satisfied to live in Egypt, make a new history, and forget the old past.

Why wasn't that good enough for God?

Joseph's purpose is to create a new life. God's purpose is to create a new nation to show that His sanctifying love can unite shattered lives and that the Sabbath can come to broken homes.

He wants to show that His love can empower you to live both through the pits of life as well as the pinnacles.

These are the two tests of faith:

1. When circumstances turn against you, and the evil in the world shatters you, will it break your spirit and make you let go of God?

2. Or when circumstances change and life gives you power, wealth, and prestige, will you give them to God and use them for His glory?

Joseph has passed the test of the pits. He has held onto God and refused to doubt His love. Now it is time for the pinnacles.

The seven years of plenty come to an end, and the prophecy of the famine becomes reality. It impacts the household of Jacob and sets the stage for the most difficult journey Joseph and his brothers will ever take—the journey to sanctification..

When the food supply grows thin, Jacob, in his same demeaning way, chides his sons, "Why are you staring at one another? There is grain in the land of Egypt, so do something for a change."

So the brothers set out to buy grain unknowingly from the last person they would ever expect to meet. When they arrived, Joseph recognized them, just as they had recognized his coat of many colors coming over the hill into their encampment and it had stirred all of their feelings. Joseph experienced the same reaction as he recognizes his ten brothers in the line of people requesting to buy grain.

"When Joseph saw his brothers, he recognized them, but he disguised himself to them and spoke to them harshly. Where have you come from? They replied, "From the land of Canaan to buy food." Although Joseph recognized his brothers, they did not recognized him. And Joseph remembered his dreams about his brothers and said to them, 'You are spies. You have come to look at the undefended parts of our land.'"

Why did Joseph take this approach?

I believe he was struggling with the hurt that every person who has been abused experiences. Memories of the hurt that these brothers have inflicted upon him pull him toward revenge, while the Spirit of God whispers forgiveness.

Can you relate to Joseph's struggles?

Seven years of good times had not erased the pain of the bad times. He did not want to see those faces that had screamed death and scowled hatred. But there they were, and they didn't have a clue that he had their lives in his hand. How ironic. How things had changed. The last time he saw them, he was pleading for his life. He was in the bottom of a pit asking them to let him go, not to hurt him, not to sell him.

Now as they approach him, they fall face down, and another memory flashes to the forefront. The dream of sheaves. When he first told it to them, they responded with, "In your dreams?" From then on, whenever they had a chance, they called him the dreamer. The syllables were saturated with sarcasm as they delivered the term. Their eyes flashed with resentment. But now the dream is fulfilled!

The struggle begins. As revenge rushes through his entire body, Joseph speaks harshly to them, positions them for justice, and sets the perfect trap. He accuses them of warlike activities, which entitles him to be able to execute them if he chooses. Now he has the legal right to exact revenge and call it justice. He can gain revenge under the guise of protecting the nation.

The brothers protest, and in the process, their response reveals that they have a father back home and a younger brother. The plot thickens as Joseph is able to snare them into another double bind. To prove that they are not spies, they must send one of them to go and get their younger brother and bring him back, while the rest of them stay there in prison. Before they can respond to his proposal, he orders them thrown into prison, where they sit for three days. That three days serves as a cooling-off period for Joseph.

I believe that this is when he drew strength from his home and from his God to walk the path of sanctification, for when he took them out of prison on the third day, he said, "Do this and live, for I fear God."

Sanctification is far from realized. Joseph still keeps the option of revenge alive, but he proposes a completely different solution. Instead of ten staying and one going home, he proposes that one should stay and nine return home to get their youngest brother Benjamin and prove that they are not spies.

God wrestled with Joseph to give him a forgiving heart.

Are you wrestling with God about forgiveness?

What brokenness does He want to heal?

What revenge does He want to replace with forgiveness?

I am sure that for Joseph, the thought of forgiving his brothers had been accepted in the same vein as wiping out a bad memory and starting over. He wanted no contact with his past—it was too painful. His hope and energy were focused on building a new future, and things were going just fine. Although he may have longed to see his father, it was not worth being subjected to his brothers. He had taken a "forgive and let live" approach. But God was opening the path of sanctification, to invite him to unify the family.

Imagine how difficult this must have been for Joseph. Think of a person who has hurt you. It's hard enough to forgive them and forget the past, but to actually think of being best friends and building a future together—that is unthinkable. Yet that is exactly what God had in mind for Joseph, for that is the power of sanctifying love. It does not simply lead us to sign a peace treaty with our enemies and to end the war, but it calls us to come together as children of God.

The highest hope we have for peace in the Middle East is simply lack of war. Stop the shooting, the treachery, the conflict. No more death and destruction. But no one has yet proposed that these people should love one another so they can build a new life of unity and brotherhood.

Yet that is exactly what the Sabbath calls us to do each week, as sanctifying love unites us as brothers and sisters in the family of God. Sabbath is the day for uniting all that has been divided. It reaches across the chasm of culture, race, gender, and even religion to bring us together, that we may become "one new humanity."

It is more than a fantasy—it is love's most powerful miracle. Jesus left His quarreling disciples with the command to "love one another as I have loved you, and by this will all men know that you are my disciples." After His death, they came to sanctifying unity in the upper room, and the Spirit filled their lives. They went into the streets—not Jews or Gentiles, men or women—but Christians set apart by unity. Love for God had created a whole new world order, where the goal was not king but servant, and their world did not begin with their own needs but the needs of others. Sanctification turns your world upside down, and it did the same for Joseph. But it is not instant or overnight—it takes time for love to transform.

It is akin to turning a caterpillar into a butterfly, as opposed to turning a frog into a prince. The transformation is just as dramatic, but the process is not instant. Sanctification is love's cocoon that embraces our ugly reality and morphs us into butterflies of grace. The other is a Cinderella fairytale where you escape from a bad home with a wicked step-mother and ugly sisters by being instantly transformed into a princess, courtesy of a fairy godmother. Where you marry a handsome prince and live happily ever after. Where you make your former taskmasters your servants. Where you never have to learn to love your enemies. On the other hand, sanctification brings love out of hate and unity out of brokenness. But it takes time! For Joseph, this phase of the struggle will take almost a year. Genesis 42:22.

Do you have someone it's difficult for you to forgive and love?

And when the brothers heard the proposal, they accepted it gladly, but they also began to break into conversation in their Hebrew tongue, and Joseph overheard these words: "Truly we are guilty concerning our brother, because we saw the distress of his soul when he pleaded with us, and yet we would not listen. Therefore, the distress is come upon us. Reuben said, 'Did I not tell you, do not sin against the boy, and you would not listen? Now comes the reckoning for his blood.'"

The interaction so touched Joseph that he turned away and wept, but he did not reveal himself. In fact, he stepped out of the room to regain his composure and returned, for the process of sanctification is one in which you let go of revenge step by step in order to embrace those who have harmed you.

It is not something that happens in a Cinderella moment. It is something that happens in a sanctified lifetime, for you never know when a cruel and uncaring action will reopen an old wound and ignite the urge to lash out. And Joseph was just beginning the journey. The first step is to begin to see the good in your enemies.

After he dried his eyes, regained his composure, and rejoined his brothers, he took Simeon from them and bound him before their eyes. They interpreted this through the eyes of their past sin, and Joseph added to that interpretation by selecting Simeon, for Simeon was the one who wanted to kill him. He was the one who instigated the plot to take his life. The firstborn, Reuben, had resisted. Judah, the fourth in line, had suggested selling him. Simeon was the hardliner who wanted his life. It would be Simeon who would sit in jail.

As Simeon was bound in front of them, not a word was spoken, but the body language and the eye contact was filled with terror, for if God was going to truly pay them back for their worst intentions, death would be their destiny. Joseph, why not stop right now and reveal yourself? Reuben has already said that they shouldn't have done this terrible thing to you. It has touched your heart, Joseph. Why continue?

It takes time to walk the road of forgiveness, and the option of revenge is always in play. Joseph is in control, and when you are in control, it is easy to let the guilty twist in the wind and watch them feel a little bit of the pain that they have so gleefully delivered.

So Joseph gave orders to fill their bags with grain and to put each man's money back in his sack, and they left. On their return home, the brothers replayed the strange encounter with the Governor of Egypt, never realizing the true plot. The next twist in the story came when they stopped to feed the animals. They opened one of the sacks of grain, only to make a surprising discovery. "'My money has been returned, and behold, it is even in my sack.' And their hearts sank, and they turned trembling to one another saying, 'What is this that God has done to us?'" For all they know, the governor is simply an agent of God returning judgment upon them for their past sins.

Throughout this story, Joseph's brothers always interpret present problems from the perspective of past sins. It is obvious that they are in need of forgiveness, for memories of their mistakes have haunted their minds, and they are held captive by the shackles of recollection. The inner expectation that justice would be served caused them to interpret every problem, every tragedy, every calamity from the perspective of the pit. Memory became their hall of justice—and sin their prosecutor.

The devil uses the sins of the past to color the present with fear and the future with anxiety, draining us of joy and hope, keeping us imprisoned by memories that we cannot forget.

In this dramatic incident, we see the contrast of the two barriers to forgiveness—revenge and guilt. Joseph struggles with revenge. The brothers struggle with guilt. They feel they should be punished. They are held captive by their past mistakes, unable to see the future except through their worst behavior of the past. Unable to believe that they could be forgiven, unable to forgive themselves, they walk the gray path of existence far from the sunlight of living and shrouded by the dusk of dying.

The brothers' guilt is compounded by the belief that God has put them in this "no-win" situation. They know that Simeon will remain in jail if they do not return, and they realize that they must return with Benjamin, the prized son of their aging father. They recognize that the money in their sacks means that they will not only return as suspected spies but as documented thieves.

They have been framed. The trap is set, and they know it!

By contrast, Joseph, who was sold into slavery, has been released from the past. God has given him the firstborn of grace, Manasseh, and he has forgotten the trouble of his family. His brothers are sin slaves, and it rules them from the throne room of their minds with condemnation, guilt, and fear.

They return to their father Jacob. Amidst this environment of depression, they eke out their existence, slowly consuming the grain. The supply dwindles; they face the inevitable. They must return to face the judgment of the governor. Genesis 43:9.

Finally Jacob says, "Go back and buy us a little food." Judah reminds him, "We cannot go back unless we take Benjamin with us." Jacob assaults their judgment for ever having disclosed they have a younger brother. The fractured family environment flares, and harsh words fly. And finally, Judah steps forward to guarantee the return of Benjamin. He asserts, "I will be surety for him. You may hold me responsible. If I do not bring him back to you and set him before you, then let me bear the blame before you forever." Genesis 43:13, 14.

Jacob loads them up with gifts for the governor and instructs them to return twice the amount of money that was put into the top of their sacks, so that there would be no question that they were willing to return the money plus interest. He sent them on their way with these words, "Take your brother also. Arise and return to the man, and may God Almighty grant you compassion in the sight of the man and he release to you your other brother and Benjamin. As for me, if I am bereaved of my children, I am bereaved."

The size of the problem is measured by the name that Jacob uses to address God. He calls upon *El Shaddai*—God Almighty. El Shaddai is the name God used when He promised Abraham that He would give him a son, Isaac. It was the name He used when Abraham believed that he was too old and that Sarah was far beyond the capability of bearing a child—that the biological barriers made the promise impossible.

If we read between the lines, Jacob is calling upon the same name for God because he believes these circumstances are almost impossible. In fact, he is setting his expectations for disaster. He says, "If I am bereaved, I am bereaved." Hardly a description of the best outcome. Rather, it is an anticipation of the worst. Even though he has invoked the most powerful God Almighty to act on his behalf, he expects that sin will have its day one more time, and his family will be shattered once again.

They leave, expecting the worst, but when they arrive, they are met with the best.

As they approach the steward of Joseph's house, they begin by trying to give the money back to him. His response is, "Be at ease. Do not be afraid. Your God and the God of your father has given your treasure in your sacks, and I have your money." Genesis 43:23.

He has obviously been instructed to make these comments. Joseph has decided not to spring the money trap. Instead, they were treated like special guests of Joseph's house and provided with all the amenities. One pleasant surprise after another sets them at ease, and when Joseph arrives home, they bow before him and give him the gifts Jacob had sent with them. He inquires about his father—he is assured that his father is doing well. His eyes scan the other brothers to find Benjamin, and when he recognizes his face, he inquires, "Is this your youngest brother of whom you spoke to me?" Being assured of that, he says, "May God be gracious to you my son." Genesis 43:29.

Joseph then hurried out, because he was deeply [disturbed] over his brother, and he sought a place to weep. He went into his bedchamber, and he wept there. The sight of Benjamin stirred the deepest of memories. It was a far different response from the one he had when he saw them without Benjamin. Memories of the love of his mother and the companionship of his younger brother swept over him, but he chose not to reveal his identity just yet.

What more could he be waiting for? What struggles still raged within the heart of Joseph? Was he simply testing his brothers to determine if they had changed, to reveal their present character, or was his character also involved in the test? Was he still struggling with revenge?

Joseph washes his face and regains control. He returns and gives the command to serve the meal, for he has yet to spring all the psychological surprises he has planned while they were away. First, he seats the brothers according to their birthright order, and the eye contact between the brothers signals astonishment. What is going on? What is happening now?

Everything was going so well, but suddenly anxiety returns as Joseph begins the mind games. The food is served, and Benjamin receives the favored portions. The meal proceeds absolutely without a hitch, and soon the brothers' anxiety dissipates and they are told that they can return home. Their donkeys have been loaded with grain, and they are free to go.

They leave the city praising God. The very best has become their lot, and as they clear the city gates, they breathe a sigh of relief and head toward home. But then the unexpected happens. They hear the sound of thundering hoofs and turn to see the palace guard headed by Joseph's steward pursuing them at full speed.

As the steward dismounts, he speaks the script Joseph has written.

"Why have you repaid evil for good? You have stolen the special cup that my lord uses for divination. You have done wrong." Genesis 44:5.

Unaware that Joseph ordered that cup to be put into Benjamin's sack, unaware that he has also placed the money in his sack, unaware that brother has framed brother, their response is absolute, certain denial. "We can guarantee that this is not true. If anyone has done it, let him die, and the rest of us will be slaves." The stakes are set—death and slavery are the self-proclaimed judgment.

They are so certain of the care they have taken to make sure that every action is appropriate. They are anxious to vindicate themselves, and then the suggestion is made that they should open their sacks. Eagerly they line up and begin to tear them open. Nothing is found until they come to Benjamin's sack. And as it is opened, the cup is revealed. They are absolutely dumbfounded, astounded, and terrified, for they realize they have been framed and that someone is out to get them.

They tear their clothes, a symbol of the distress of their spirit. They reload the donkeys and return in mourning to the governor's palace. Judah leads the way, for he is the one who has provided the assurance, and when they arrive, he falls to the ground before Joseph, who is undaunted by their distress. Fully composed, he asks, "What is this deed that you have done? Do you not know that such a man as I can indeed practice divination?"

And Judah said, "What can we say to you, my lord, and what can we speak, and how can we justify ourselves? God has found out the iniquity of your servants." Genesis 44:16.

Apparently the ride back had been filled with conversation regarding how they should relate to the situation. They interpreted all these calamities as paybacks for their misdeeds to Joseph, and when Judah fell down before him, he offered no defense. He confessed his sin. In fact, he called it the worst type of sin—iniquity. Iniquity is conscious rebellion—calculated evil.

It really did not reference the sin of the cup, for in fact, Benjamin was without fault. They all were. There was no sin on their part. If sin had occurred there, it was Joseph's sin, but the sin that Judah was referencing was the iniquity against Joseph.

Judah takes the most dramatic step on behalf of all of his brothers to release them from the past, by confessing that the sin against their brother had been iniquity. No defense, no explanation—simply open confession. You cannot forgive yourself until you have faced yourself and confessed before God the depth of your mistake.

Joseph's response is pointed. It drives the agenda further and deeper, and he says, "Far be it from me to enslave you all. The man in whose possession the cup has been found, he shall be my slave, but as for you, go in peace to your father."

Now Judah takes the second step in breaking the barrier of forgiveness, and he asks to approach Joseph. He comes close, both in person and in spirit, as he reveals the motivation of his heart by his request. He explains that his father will die if this boy is not returned. He recites his promise to bring back the younger brother, but he adds the history of Joseph to the conversation and says, "And your servant, my father, said to us, 'You know that my wife bore me two sons, and one went out from me, and I said surely he is torn in pieces and I have not seen him since. If you take this one also from me and harm befalls him, he will bring my gray head down to [the grave] in sorrow.'" Genesis 44:21-29.

Now Judah requests that his life might redeem Benjamin's life. Judah, the forefather of the Messiah, the Saviour of the world, takes on the messianic role of redeemer. He offers himself as a substitute: "Now, therefore, please let your servant remain instead of the lad, a slave to my lord, and let the lad go with his brothers." Genesis 44:33.

Joseph's eyes filled with tears, his lips began to quiver, and he wept uncontrollably, loud and long. Judah's substitutional sacrifice had freed Joseph's heart of any inclination for revenge, he was overcome by the spirit of redemption, and the loudness of his weeping reflected the depths of his pain. Through crying, he began to release the brokenness of his past, that God might heal the present and unite the future and create the family of Israel. Joseph and Judah model sanctification's unifying power and create the foundation for making one nation great.

24

Seeing Providence in Pain

JOSEPH'S NEXT STEP IS FULL of drama and instruction. He orders everyone to leave him alone with his brothers. "So there was no man with him when Joseph made himself know to his brothers." Sanctifying love works the miracle of reconciliation in the privacy of personal confession and forgiveness. Genesis 45:1.

Joseph knows that public confession often results in focusing on the sin that separates, when their only hope for becoming family is to focus on the love that forgives and forgets.

Joseph is following the principle that Jesus outlined in Matthew 18:15: "If your bother sins, go and reprove him in private." This story would have made headline news in the Egyptian press, and Joseph knew it. But public sensation often leads to humiliation. Humility must be embraced by all, but humiliation must be experienced by none.

The circle of confession needs to be no wider than the circle of offense. Confession is for those who have broken hearts, not for those who have curious ears. Joseph knew that the family circle must be respected in order to be restored.

The brothers watched as the entourage of servants and officials left the room and silent tears cascaded down Joseph's face. The moments must have seemed like hours as they wondered what would happen next. "So when they were all alone, Joseph made himself known to his brothers." It was the last possible scenario they had imagined, yet it was also their worst fear come true. Suddenly all the pieces of the puzzle began to fall together, and their anxiety moved to terror.

This explains why the money was in the sack. This explains why he asked about our father. This explains Simeon. This explains the way we were seated at the table. This explains the five portions for Benjamin, and this explains the cup in Benjamin's sack. This explains it all. This is the dreamer—and we are living the fulfillment of the dream. We are dead men!

They were ready to be judged by God, but they had no idea that the twist of providence would place them face to face with their brother. Knowing his nature and their own, they stood speechless, absolutely gripped by fear, shock, and dismay.

Joseph persuades them to come closer, and they respond. He confirms their fears, "I am your brother, Joseph," he begins, "whom you sold into Egypt." Genesis 45:4.

It's him, alright. He remembers being sold. Yes, he's got the facts. Now it was their turn to cry, but he interrupts, "Do not be grieved or angry with yourselves because you sold me here, for God sent me before you to preserve life." Genesis 45:5.

Joseph deals with the two most common emotions we face when we are confronted with our mistakes: grief and anger. *Grief* is the personal emotion that we turn inward in humiliation when engulfed by sorrow and shame. We can't believe that we have done such an evil—it attacks our self worth as we realize the kind of person we have become. Grief turns inward to mourn the death of our self image. *Anger,* on the other hand, punishes the spirit, lashing it with self-inflicted criticism, calling it before the judgment bar of the mind, serving as judge and jury to self-convict. It sentences one to self-hatred.

Are you trying to cope with grief or anger in your life?

Both reactions—grief and anger—only lead down the path of separation, punctuated by statements such as, "I can't bear to face that person again." "I can't even think of going back to church after this." When we torture ourselves with grief and anger, we are in danger of never finding the road to forgiveness. These are the devil's detours that lead us to the antisocial cul-de-sacs of self-inflicted depression.

Don't go on the detours of grief or anger. Walk the road of forgiveness and reinterpret life's events. Yes, you made a mistake. We have all made mistakes, but it doesn't mean that we can never get back together. God has the ability to re-weave the torn fabric of our family with the thread of forgiveness. It will start with a new perspective—a perspective Joseph had gained from his seventeen years of adversity. "God sent me before you to preserve life."

Instead of blaming his brothers, he credits God. Instead of repeating the fact that he was sold, he says that he was sent. Instead of defining his exile as persecution, he calls it preservation. Instead of defining his work as simply survival, he calls it life.

It is amazing how the miracle of forgiveness starts with reframing our circumstances. God gifts us with wisdom to see our world through God's eyes and reinterprets the facts around God's saving acts. He saves us from revenge that we may reach out instead of lash out. He saves us from brokenness that we may be made whole. His blood rewrites history, that we may make history. He unites us with our unloved ones, that His love may create family and preserve life.

Are you in need of experiencing forgiveness?

The mile markers of forgiveness mark the road of life. It is a road of continual repentance and renewal. Forgiveness is not an occasion—it is a lifestyle. When you look at your worst tragedies through God's eyes, you have the potential to reinterpret your scars.

Joseph says, "Let's face the facts. You sold me, but God sent me." There is no glossing over of their intentions, but there is the statement of a higher reality that all things can work together for good for them that love God. He goes on to explain that the famine will last another five years. This tells us that it took two years of famine before the story was completely played out.

Joseph continues, "God sent me before you to preserve for you a remnant in the earth and to keep you alive by a great deliverance." A deliverance from the famine of the land that threatened to starve them physically—and a deliverance from the famine of the soul that threatened to starve them spiritually.

Joseph repeats, "Now, therefore, it was not you who sent me here, but God." It is as if he is reminding himself of his chosen interpretation as opposed to his natural interpretation. Sanctification builds its greatest monuments on the soil of our deepest hurts. Forgiveness is the glue of love that restores broken dreams and enables us to live again.

Joseph now realizes why all of these events have happened in this fashion and framework. Suddenly the dreams of the past make sense. It was not a dream about Joseph rising to greatness and his brothers recognizing it through humility. It was a dream of God bringing him to greatness. It was a dream about the greatness of God, not the greatness of Joseph.

God is so great! He can break the barriers of biology and bring the promised child to an infertile couple long beyond the age of childbearing. God is so great! He can take the child who has been shamed and never known a father's love and bless him with a new name—or give her the Messiah of hope. God is so great! He can heal a dysfunctional family racked with abuse and violence. God is so great! His love can create a chosen nation out of a broken home. GOD IS SO GREAT!

25

Finally Family

THERE IS NO MORE POWERFUL WITNESS than when God heals a family, whether it is between a husband and wife, or as in this case, between siblings. The author of Genesis gives us a snapshot of sanctification's healing power. It stands in stark contrast to the description of the dysfunctional family who hated Joseph and could not speak "a kind word to him." Genesis 37:4.

As original love resets the broken relationship, Joseph and his brothers are wrapped in a tearful embrace. Then the author inserts these words: "Afterward his brothers talked with him." What a contrast from hatred to embrace, from glares of hatred to tears of forgiveness, from angry words to kind conversation.

The scene reminds me of Paul's prayer. "I bow my knees before the Father, from whom every family in heaven and on earth derives its name, and pray that He would grant you, according to the riches of His glory, to be strengthened with power through His Spirit abiding in each of you." Ephesians 3:14-16.

This day these brothers became family and began a great nation. And the history of the nation would testify to the power of sanctification to mend broken hearts and to cleanse bitter spirits. The nation of Israel would include all of the brothers—there would be no distinction drawn between the sons of Leah and the sons of Rachel. The nation would eventually be split into two kingdoms— Judah and Israel. It would not split along bloodlines, and that is a testimony to the healing power of sanctification.

Contrast this to the sons of Abraham—Isaac and Ishmael. The enmity between these two brothers has been imbedded in religious, genealogical, and geographical differences that have cost millions of lives. Although the differences are ancient, the hatred is current. The Middle East has become the hotbed for conflict that threatens to engulf the world. Family feuds are the real basis of much of our world's violence, and that is why this story is such a testimony and model for us today. It documents a peace that only God can bring through Sabbath.

The miracle of sanctification is newsworthy and bears witness to the power of original love It won the heart of Pharaoh.

He was pleased by what he heard, and he gave Joseph a message. "Say to your brothers, 'Do this, load your beasts, and go back to the land of Canaan and take your father and household and come to me and I will give you the best of the land of Egypt, and you shall eat the fat of the land.'" Genesis 45:19, 20.

Pharaoh was so impressed with the story that he commanded that a lavish train of provisions be sent to announce the good news to an aging father that his favorite son Joseph was still alive and well in Egypt.

So now the brothers prepare to leave, faced with a new dilemma. What will they say to their father? How are they going to explain that Joseph is alive? How wide should the circle of confession go? It could be an issue of great debate and contention.

But Joseph admonishes them, "Do not quarrel on the journey." Another translation of this is, "Do not be agitated with each other on the journey." Joseph knew that his brothers would have to complete both a physical and spiritual journey to reach home. Joseph's sanctification struggle was between revenge and forgiveness. His brothers' struggle would be between repentance and rationalization, confession and deception.

Each brother's contemplations on the way home might be something like this: *"OK, the technical truth is that Joseph is alive. Do we need to make a full disclosure of everything? Do we come clean with the facts that we sold him into slavery and deceived our family with a bloody coat and a lion tale? We caused twenty years of grief and maintained it with twenty years of lies. How can we confess it all?*

It would be a hard journey home, yet sanctification must work into every crack of our broken lives before it can work out unifying love. Truth must fully excavate the landscape of our relationships in order to build family trust.

One real source of agitation would be in agreeing how to announce the news that Joseph is alive and well to their aging father. There was an abundance of other good news. Simeon had been released. Benjamin was safe, and all of the riches of Egypt were laid at their disposal to rescue them from the famine in the land.

Joseph knew his brothers. He knew the flash points in their relationships. He knew that the trip home would be needed to allow them time to process all the events that had taken place. Time to fill the gap between living and lying. Time to commit to the Lord of truth. Time to spiritually traverse the divide between their old world of blame and their new world of sanctification. Time to fill the gaps in their relationships and to pray and talk through how to bring sanctification to the rest of their family.

The trip home marked the beginning of a different kind of family journey—a journey to unity. Sanctification must break through the walls that have been built around hearts. It must open the closed door of compassion that has been locked tight by bitterness. Forgetting is a human impossibility without forgiveness. And unity is impossible without healing. This is the journey that will create the bond of Sabbath love and make the nation great!

By the time they arrived in Canaan, they had determined how they would present the news to their father. Truth won out, and they announced, "Joseph is still alive, and indeed he is ruler over all the land of Egypt."

Jacob was so stunned that he wouldn't believe them. So, patiently, they went through the whole story and retold the actual dialogue with Joseph as he had told them about all the ways that God had provided for him. When Jacob saw the wagons from Pharaoh arriving, he believed them and said, "It is enough. My son Joseph is still alive, and I will go and see him before I die!"

There is no record of the brothers' confession. One can only infer that it must have taken place. The greatest evidence is found in the blessing that Israel gave Joseph, recorded in Genesis 49:22, 23. Commentators believe that Israel disguised the incident in this metaphor: "Joseph is a fruitful bough, a fruitful bough by a spring; its branches run over the wall. The archers bitterly attacked him, And shot at him and harassed him; but his bow remained unyielding."

Scripture sometimes preserves private moments of reconciliation by excluding them from the record. Israel limits the understanding of the brothers' treachery by couching it in terms they would understand but that others may not. The glory of God is to cover sin—the effort of man is to cover up sin.

Humans love to read the story behind the story and savor the sordid details of evil exposed. God loves to bring out Himself in us. "Christ in you the hope of glory" God loves to spend time remembering how He worked in us to bring about good, as opposed to how sin worked in us to bring about evil.

God delights in blotting out sin. "I am the one who wipes out your transgressions for My own sake; and I will not remember your sins." Isaiah 43:25. By nature, God is focused on sanctification, and by nature, we are focused on blame. God CAN remember our sins—He does not have celestial Alzheimer's. He simply chooses to focus on love. And He promises that if we are willing to ask forgiveness, He will help us rewrite history, starting with a heavenly eraser. He loves to recreate Sabbath in our broken lives as He did among the family of Jacob-Israel!

The Return to Egypt

As the caravan entered Egypt, "Joseph prepared his chariot and went up to Goshen to meet his father Israel; as soon as he appeared before him, he embraced him and wept for a long time." They were finally family.

For seventeen years the children of Israel lived and worked together in the lush land of Goshen. Scripture says that they were fruitful and multiplied. This was the Ephraim period of their family life. But it seemed almost too good to be true. Sabbath is often that way. When it works out God's original plan in our lives and unites us in love, and we are together with God and family, we wonder how long it will last.

If the devil can't convince us that what God has promised is a lie, then he whispers that it won't last. That is what he did with the brothers. When Jacob died, they questioned whether sanctification would turn back to blame. They came up with a scheme to test the lasting power of sanctification. "When Joseph's brothers saw that their father was dead, they said, 'What if Joseph should bear a grudge against us and pay us back in full for all the wrong which we did to him!'"

It's hard for humans to believe that God's sanctifying love can change a person so that they no longer carry a grudge. "So they sent a message to Joseph, saying, 'Your father left this message before he died, "Please forgive, I beg you, the transgression of your brothers and their sin, for they did you wrong." And now, please forgive the transgression of the servants of the God of your father.'"

When Joseph heard the message, he began weeping. It is a replay of the scene of their reconciliation almost eighteen years earlier. Think of all the ways he could have reacted. No doubt he knew the brothers were making up the message to save their own lives and representing it as their father's last words to manipulate the situation for their advantage. How tempting it would be to believe that they had not really changed and that for the last seventeen years their actions had really been prompted by fear and not love. When someone you love disappoints you by bringing up the past when you thought it was over and done, it is a moment of truth.

Has someone ever disappointed you this way?

The brothers must have been waiting just outside, because when they heard Joseph weeping, they rushed into the room and fell down before him, saying, "Behold, we are your servants." But Joseph said to them, "Do not be afraid, for am I in God's place?"

Joseph will not indulge in judgment, paying back slavery with slavery. God has granted him the position of judge over the earthly kingdom of Egypt, but he has not been called to exercise eternal judgment. Joseph does not confuse earthly status and authority with heavenly status and authority. God alone is the one to judge, and Joseph refuses to play God's role on earth.

Assuming God's role by judging others is what divides families and churches. God said that He sent Jesus to save the world as opposed to condemning it. Jesus advised His followers: "Judge not so you will not be held accountable for judging."

The goal of original love is to unify—the effect of original sin is to divide. First, sin gets us to stray from God, and then, to judge others, dividing us from our Father and then from our family.

Whenever the devil tempts us to judge others, we must realize that there is only one who has the right to judge sinners—and it is the one who died for them. Jesus went to heaven to judge only after He came to earth to die. Before He ascended to the seat of judgment, He hung on the cross of mercy. This is why you can trust the judgment, because you have witnessed the love of the judge. This is why no one can ever think to take God's place. When tempted to judge, remember Joseph's words, "Am I God to you?"

In my role as an administrator, I am called to discipline but not judge. Someone may need to change an attitude or role in the organization, but that change must be done in a manner that treats the person as a child of God. In situations where I have remembered this, I have advanced sanctification in Florida Hospital and in my life personally. When I have forgotten, I need forgiveness that I may always remember that my calling is not to divide the sheep and the goats but to call them to the Shepherd.

The story closes as Joseph comforts his brothers with these words: "Do not be afraid; I will provide for you and your little ones. So he comforted them and spoke kindly to them."

Sanctification is not too good to be true. But it is beyond the comprehension of a broken world trapped in a cycle of violence and revenge. Joseph's life is a shining example of what can happen when a person allows God to recreate Sabbath in the midst of brokenness.

Step into the sanctuary of Sabbath. Let the Father mend your heart and fill it with His love. Then you can walk out into the world and reach out with forgiving love to your worst enemy. It is truly possible that in His time He will restore waht sin has broken. He will make you fruitful in the land of affliction. So step into the sanctuary of Sabbath.

Step into the sanctuary of Sabbath. God waits there for broken people to bring the pieces of their world to Him that He might turn them into peace. Step into the sanctuary of the Sabbath, where sanctifying love offers all people the possibility of unity. Step into the sanctuary of Sabbath so you may live in His Original Love.

Experiencing
Sabbath Sanctification

SABBATH SANCTIFIED: To experience a love relationship of togetherness and harmony, appreciating the concept of being "set apart to grow together"—and as individuals and as a family, to enable us to extend this concept to others.

Examples of ways to experience Sabbath Sanctified:

1. Dedication and celebration of possessions and life events:

• Newborn—Celebrate the child's "dedication" day each year until their baptism (new clothes, small gifts, family and friends get together, and so on).

• Play items—For the young child, have separate toys/play items just for church. Keep them in a special container (such as a tote bag) with items for "quiet entertainment" while you teach the child reverence for God's house. Some items I have used: small felts with a felt board, spiritual books, colored pencils and paper, ribbons and pipe cleaners of varied colors, a picture Bible, a small purse or wallet with money for church, a small songbook. (It is important to use items that will not mess up the pews.) Many times my Sabbath Surprises were for the church bag. Rotating new or different items into the church bag will keep the child's interest and heighten anticipation.

• New home—(an example of a home dedication will be on the Website.)

• Television—stating each family member's desire to watch programs that enrich the individual and/or family.

• New furniture or purchased items for the home.

• Car keys—an example of a dedication ceremony for teens beginning to drive, illustrating the writing of a contract covenant, can be found on the Website.

• Car and glove compartment for teens (explained on Website).

• Symbols for personal reminders for youth of their commitment(s) to belong to God: cross, chain, pins, key to heart, etc. (see Website).

2. Dedication of time:

• Preparation for Sabbath: We utilize the biblical principle and process of advanced planning with Sunday calendar coordination and family tasks for each day of the week. An example of how our family plans for four Sabbaths in advance, including planning for the church service, offerings, and Sabbath afternoon activities, will be on the Website.

• Preparation for church: How to "practice" church with small kids at home. Suggested ways to assist children to be more attentive and involved in the church service (Website).

• Family talk time: Examples of our family worships and our "lights out" routine will be on the Website.

• Family connectiveness: Notes, conference calls, specific family prayer time, and ways to stay connected with the extended family (Website).

• Devotional time: Individually—and as a family (Website).

• Quiet time: Examples of this important principle for children and every family member (Website).

• Scheduled family time: Examples of family retreat and writing personal and family mission statements (see the Website).

3. Service to others: (including holidays, as below).

Examples of the following service-oriented relationship stories of our family will be on the Website:

• Younger child: regular visits to an elderly neighbor.

• Older child: retirement, nursing home visitation, adopting "grandparents."

• Teens: home love feast.

• Adult: sitting for single parents and caretakers

4. Holidays: (further explained on our Website).

• Easter—plastic egg, muffins, and the cross.

• Halloween—reverse trick or treat.

• Valentines' Day—homemade cards.

• May Day—"surprise" flowers to neighbors.

• Christmas—neighborhood caroling, Christmas card prayer tradition.

5. Family "unity" activities:

• Creating communication covenants.

• Rules for fighting fair.

• Speaking the truth in love.

You're invited to visit *originalove.com.*

Hart Research Center

Resources for the Active Church

▲ To order additional copies of this book
▲ To obtain a catalog of other Hart Research Center books and products
▲ To order the video entitled "Original Love in Action"

Contact Hart Research Center at

1-800-487-4278

or visit our website at

www.hartresearch.org